TRACING YOUR ANCESTORS IN LUNATIC ASYLUMS

FAMILY HISTORY FROM PEN & SWORD

TRACING YOUR ANCESTORS IN LUNATIC ASYLUMS

A Guide for Family Historians

Michelle Higgs

Pen & Sword
FAMILY HISTORY

First published in Great Britain in 2019
PEN & SWORD FAMILY HISTORY
an imprint of
Pen & Sword Books Ltd
47 Church Street, Barnsley, South Yorkshire, S70 2AS

ISBN 978 1 52674 485 2

Typeset in Palatino and Optima by CHIC GRAPHICS

Printed and bound in England by TJ International Ltd, Padstow, Cornwall

Pen & Sword Books Ltd incorporates the imprints of Pen & Sword
Airworld, Archaeology, Atlas, Aviation, Battleground, Discovery, Family
History, Fiction, History, Maritime, Military, Military Classics, Politics,
Select, Social History, True Crime, Frontline Books, Leo Cooper,
Remember When, Seaforth Publishing, The Praetorian Press,
Wharncliffe Local History, Wharncliffe Transport,
Wharncliffe True Crime and White Owl.

For a complete list of Pen & Sword titles please contact

PEN & SWORD BOOKS LTD
47 Church Street, Barnsley, South Yorkshire, S70 2AS, England
E-mail: enquiries@pen-and-sword.co.uk
Website: www.pen-and-sword.co.uk
or
PEN & SWORD BOOKS LTD
1950 Lawrence Rd., Havertown, PA 19083, USA
E-mail: Uspen-and-sword@casematepublishers.com
Website: www.penandswordbooks.com

CONTENTS

DEDICATION

This book is dedicated to the hundreds of thousands of people who were patients in lunatic asylums and mental hospitals before 1948 whose stories have never been told.

ACKNOWLEDGEMENTS

While writing this book, I received help and advice in locating information and illustrations from a number of different sources. I would like to express my gratitude to the following: Borthwick Institute for Archives, University of York; Alex Cox at Find My Past; Devon Archives and Local Studies Service, Exeter; Essex Record Office; Fife Archives; Gwent Archives; Liverpool Record Office; Lothian Health Services Archive; National Records of Scotland; Oxleas NHS Foundation Trust; Public Record Office of Northern Ireland; Staffordshire Record Office; Surrey History Centre; The National Archives; Jenni Trimlett at Ancestry; Wellcome Library; Wiltshire and Swindon Archives; Worcestershire Archives and Archaeology Service; and Worcestershire Health and Care NHS Trust.

Special thanks are due to: Howard Doble at London Metropolitan Archives; Colin Gale at Bethlem Museum of the Mind; Emma Maxwell at www.scottishindexes.com; Lisa Spurrier and Mark Stevens at Berkshire Record Office; and Kevin Towers of West London NHS Trust.

I would also like to thank the following people who were so generous with their time and their research: Trevor Beal, Pam Chapman, Linda Cooke, Mike Gallagher, Lindsay Hall, Sandra Halling, Carl Higgs, Pete Houghton, Walter Jenkins, Lorna Latham, Maureen Long, Howard Mais, Val Preece, Sylvia Singleton, Yvonne Spargo, Roy Tuckey, Ann Vennard, Alan Weeks and Lesley West.

I am extremely grateful to the Authors' Foundation, administered by the Society of Authors, for providing me with a generous grant, without which I could not have completed this book.

Finally, I would like to thank my husband Carl for his unfailing support, and my family and friends for their encouragement during the writing of this book.

DOCUMENTS AND ILLUSTRATIONS

Every effort has been made to trace copyright holders of images and owners of documents included in this book. The publishers would be grateful for further information concerning any image or document for which we have been unable to trace a copyright holder or owner.

INTRODUCTION

The mind is a fragile thing. It can be broken by the grief of losing a loved one, the breakdown of a marriage or relationship, or the stress and worry of making ends meet in tough economic times. It can be damaged by witnessing, or being involved in, a traumatic accident or act of war, the inability to find employment to provide for one's family, or an addiction to alcohol or drugs. These often universal human experiences were as common for our ancestors as they are in modern times, but the treatment of their mental illnesses was very different.

Today, mental health is frequently talked about in TV documentaries, newspapers and magazines, on social media and in high profile campaigns such as Time to Change and Heads Together – and rightly so. The more conversations we have about it, the better we can understand and empathise with sufferers of mental illness.

By contrast, for our ancestors, the stigma and shame of mental illness was widespread, often making it difficult for us to track them in asylums or even to know of their existence. For many people, their mentally afflicted relatives were out of sight and out of mind while they were incarcerated in an institution, a secret never to be revealed. Their names and photographs were blotted out of the family tree and the next generation was not made aware of their plight. Some children were told their mother or father had died, rather than letting them know they were a patient in an asylum.

This may appear unfeeling, unsympathetic or cruel but sometimes we can only learn half the story from the available documents and oral history. The fear of aggressive behaviour and the feeling of not being able to cope with a 'difficult' relative; wanting him or her to be in the right place to get proper treatment and care; knowing that mental illness was sometimes hereditary and could damage marriage prospects: these are just a few of the genuine reasons someone might seek help for a loved one in an asylum.

Even the terminology used to describe the insane had negative connotations; their minds were disordered, deranged or diseased. Madness was considered shameful because sufferers let go of their inhibitions and were incapable of self-control; it was therefore something for the sane to be afraid of.

The labels associated with mental illness have changed markedly since the nineteenth and early twentieth centuries. For example, the terms 'imbecile' and 'idiot' were used indiscriminately to describe anyone with a weak or feeble mind. Although these terms are now considered derogatory, they accurately reflect the attitudes of the time. Today, such people might be described as being learning disabled. Epileptics and those suffering from other conditions that caused fits were also classed in this category with the genuine mentally ill.

This book aims to give an overview of lunatic asylums in the UK from the eighteenth century up to 1948, when the National Health Service was founded. However, it will focus most closely on the Victorian era as this is the most document-rich period for researching ancestors in mental institutions.

Throughout the book, you will find case studies of real people who were patients in lunatic asylums or mental hospitals. The Sources section discusses a variety of printed records, original documents and online sources in greater detail, showing how they can be used to trace your own forebears in lunatic asylums. This book assumes you have no previous knowledge of family history, but if you already know the basics of genealogical research, simply dip into the sections you're most interested in.

As this book is not designed to be a definitive history of lunatic asylums, the bibliography lists numerous titles to increase your knowledge of the subject. They offer comprehensive research about individual asylums, types of patients or more in-depth information about the history of institutions that treated the mentally ill.

Chapter 1

CARE OF THE MENTALLY ILL BEFORE 1800

If your ancestor was afflicted with mental illness, where could their relatives turn to for help with care? Before the eighteenth century, the options were extremely limited if they came from the poorer sections of society. That's because there were no state-run asylums in Britain to treat or accommodate the mentally sick.

In fact, until the early eighteenth century, Bethlem Hospital in London was the only public institution for insane patients. Founded in 1247 as a priory of the Church of St Mary of Bethlehem, by the 1400s it was taking in small numbers of pauper lunatics in an attempt to cure them. Colloquially known as 'Bedlam', by the mid-sixteenth century, the hospital appears to have been exclusively for the insane.

In 1676, Bethlem reopened in a palatial new building situated in Moorfields, outside the City walls. Designed by architect Robert Hooke, it could accommodate 120 patients. This first purpose-built asylum became the model for the institutions that followed. On the two main floors there were individual cells measuring 12 feet by 8 feet, with straw palliasses for the patients to sleep on. Dangerous lunatics were chained in their cells day and night, whilst the more harmless inmates were allowed to use the long galleries as day rooms. In addition, there were two walled airing courts in which the patients could exercise.

Treatment involved being plunged in cold and warm baths as

Old Bethlem Hospital, Moorfields, circa 1750. (From Old and New London, *1881)*

well as blood-letting, purgatives and emetics. Paying sightseers were allowed into Bethlem to view the lunatics and Frenchman César de Saussure recorded his impressions when he visited in 1725:

> On the second floor is a corridor and cells like those on the first floor, and this is the part reserved for dangerous maniacs, most of them being chained and terrible to behold. On holidays numerous persons of both sexes, but belonging generally to the lower classes, visit this hospital, and amuse themselves watching these unfortunate wretches, who often give them cause for laughter.

The treatment of lunatics at Bethlem reflected the prevailing school of thought in the seventeenth and early eighteenth centuries. It was believed that the most effective way to control dangerous maniacs and protect the public was to confine them with strict discipline, coercion and a 'low diet'. Whilst the conditions at Bethlem were clearly spartan and the regime was harsh, it was arguably no worse than the jails and workhouses of the time.

CARE IN THE COMMUNITY

The majority of mentally ill paupers were kept at home by their immediate families and locked away in an attic or cellar if they posed a danger to themselves or others. If there were no relatives, responsibility fell on the parish, which might board him or her out to someone locally.

This was the custom in Wales, where it was common to board out idiots and lunatics with relatives, or with another person, usually a peasant or small farmer, who would look after them in return for a weekly allowance. This system of community care was known as 'farming out'. Before the nineteenth century, Scotland and Ireland also favoured out-relief, keeping insane people in their own homes wherever possible.

Another option for parishes was to incarcerate violent lunatics in a prison or bridewell. At the other end of the scale, harmless lunatics were frequently left to fend for themselves and reduced to begging in the streets.

For affluent families, there was a greater choice of care. They could pay for a doctor or clergyman to look after their loved one either in their own home or, more commonly, in a private household; the latter type of accommodation became known as a 'madhouse'. In England, small private madhouses had existed since the seventeenth century, for example, at Box in Wiltshire (circa 1615), Glastonbury (circa 1656) and Bilston, Staffordshire (circa 1700). In London, a number of madhouses were established from about 1670, particularly in the Hoxton and Clerkenwell areas.

Chancery lunatics were also frequently accommodated in English private madhouses. These were usually wealthy people who had been found insane by inquisition at the behest of their relatives or heirs. In order to stop the alleged lunatic's fortune from being squandered, the family could petition the Lord Chancellor. He could then issue a writ *'de lunatico inquirendo'*, after which the case was looked into by a jury with witnesses including physicians with experience in mental health; the alleged lunatic was also questioned. If a person was found lunatic by inquisition, their estates would then fall under the supervision of the Crown.

The process was simplified after the Lunatics' Property Act of 1842, which appointed two barristers known as Commissioners in Lunacy to protect the estates (later, they were called Masters in Lunacy).

It is difficult to say how many private madhouses were in operation in the seventeenth century since by their very nature, they were not publicised and were secretive places. The wealthy were prepared to pay high sums for absolute discretion about their insane relatives.

CHARITABLE ASYLUMS

From the eighteenth century, attitudes towards the mentally ill began to change significantly. No longer was it acceptable to view lunatics as figures of fun but confinement in asylums was considered necessary to have the best chance of curing a person's insanity.

As a result, several charitable public asylums were established in England, the first of which was Bethel Hospital in Norwich, founded in 1713; this catered for twenty to thirty patients at a time. It was to be a further forty years before other cities followed suit with their own charitable institutions for lunatics. In 1765, a subscription was begun to raise funds to build a lunatic asylum for the Newcastle, Durham and Northumberland areas; this asylum was opened in Newcastle two years later. Manchester's Lunatic Hospital was founded in 1766 on a site next to the city's infirmary, with twenty-two cells. Before the end of the eighteenth century, charitable lunatic asylums were also established at Liverpool, York, Hereford, Leicester and Exeter, as well as the York Retreat for Quakers (1796).

Conditions in some of these early charitable asylums were rudimentary at best. For example, the *Historical Account of Newcastle upon Tyne including the Borough of Gateshead*, published in 1827, described Newcastle's first lunatic asylum as:

> but ill calculated to answer the purposes of such an hospital. It was frequently crowded to excess, and little attention was paid to free ventilation and cleanliness. The chains, iron bars and dungeon-like cells presented to the unhappy inmates all the irritating and melancholy characteristics of a prison, and, at the same time, were highly injurious to their health and lives. Many of the cells were close, dark, cold holes (less comfortable than cow-houses), the doors of which opened direct upon a court-yard. There was no proper classification observed, and occasionally both males and females were mixed together; while, in the medical treatment of the patients, the old and exploded system of restraint and coercion was pursued.

Despite these less than salubrious surroundings, by 1817, Newcastle Asylum had treated 402 patients, 158 of whom were cured, while forty-nine were better.

In London, provision was being made for those with incurable lunacy who had no relatives to look after them. At Bethlem, the building was extended in 1723 and 1736 to accommodate these patients. However, most lunatics treated there only stayed for a year or less. A ward for incurable lunatics was also established in 1728 at Guy's Hospital.

In 1751, St Luke's Hospital was opened in the capital as a public lunatic asylum. This was an alternative to Bethlem and was founded by physician William Battie, who was critical of Bethlem's practices. St Luke's was billed as a more humane establishment with occupational therapy and less coercion and bleeding. From the beginning, paying sightseers were not allowed. In *A Treatise on*

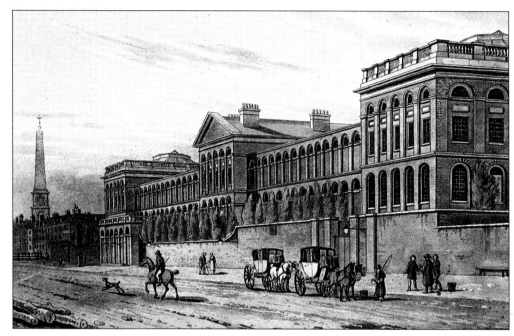

St Luke's Hospital, Cripplegate, London: the facade from the east. Coloured aquatint after T.H. Shepherd, 1815. (Wellcome Collection. CC BY)

Madness (1758), Battie wrote that 'the impertinent curiosity of those, who think it pastime to converse with madmen and to play upon their passions, ought strictly to be forbidden.' He argued that, if handled humanely, lunacy was 'no less curable than any other disease'. After 1770, Bethlem had forbidden casual gawping visitors to the hospital; tickets were issued instead, which had to be signed by a governor.

Later in the century, the 'madness' of King George III and the harsh treatment he received brought mental illness to the attention of the public. The king had suffered a short breakdown in 1765 and later experienced periods of derangement followed by remission in 1788, 1801, 1804 and 1810. In the last decade of his life, he developed dementia, which led to the establishment of the Regency.

THE 'TRADE IN LUNACY'

In the eighteenth and early nineteenth centuries, the number of private madhouses in England increased steadily to meet the demand of the so-called 'trade in lunacy'. They operated on a profit basis within the free market economy, and their size and standard of care varied considerably. Most took pauper lunatics as well as private patients, their fees being paid by the parish or Poor Law union that had sent them.

Some private madhouses were huge establishments, such as Haydock Lodge in Lancashire, licensed for 400 pauper and fifty private patients, and Warburton's White House in Bethnal Green, where, in 1815, there were a total of 360 patients, of whom 230 were paupers. These large-scale institutions were, however, exceptions to the rule. In 1800, there were just seven asylums outside the capital with more than thirty patients, and between ten and twenty with fewer.

While some establishments were run by lay proprietors, the most sought after and expensive were superintended by medical professionals, such as Thomas Arnold MD's Belle Grove Asylum in Leicester and Nathaniel Cotton MD's 'Collegium Insanorum' in St Albans. Founded in about 1745, Cotton's madhouse catered for no more than half a dozen patients at a time, charging from three to five guineas a week, so clearly he was targeting the wealthy lunatic. The poet William Cowper was a patient there from 1763 to 1765 after several suicide attempts. He praised the asylum and its staff in his autobiography, especially Dr Cotton, who was 'ever watchful and apprehensive for my welfare'.

Few private madhouses were purpose-built, with the majority being adapted from large houses. Notable exceptions include the York Retreat, Brislington House near Bristol and Ticehurst House in East Sussex, one of the most superior madhouses. Founded in 1792 by surgeon-apothecary Samuel Newington, patients at Ticehurst could live in separate villas in the grounds, bring their own cooks and even ride to hounds. As Roy Porter points out in *Madmen*, the trade in lunacy 'produced palaces as well as pigsties'.

By the 1760s, there were calls to fully regulate madhouses in order to stamp out the worst abuses. Wrongful confinement of the sane was one such issue. There's no evidence to suggest this happened on a large scale, but when occurrences came to light, they made headline news. One such case involved an alleged lunatic named Mrs Deborah D'Vebre. In 1761, she had been confined at Robert Turlington's madhouse in Chelsea by her husband. Her relatives brought the case to court and a doctor was allowed to see Mrs D'Vebre at the asylum. He reported that she was 'absolutely free from the least appearance of insanity' and she was subsequently released. Two years later, *The Gentleman's Magazine* condemned the 'many unlawful, arbitrary, cruel and oppressive acts' committed in private madhouses and pleaded for regulation of such establishments.

However, it was to be another eleven years before the government acted. Under the Madhouses Act of 1774, all private madhouses in England and Wales had to be licensed by magistrates, and their annual licences could only be renewed if admission registers had been properly maintained. Madhouses outside the capital were visited by Justices of the Peace accompanied by a medical practitioner, whilst in London, the inspecting body was the Royal College of Physicians. However, the most important part of the Act was that which insisted on medical certification for all patients, except paupers. This gave some protection to sane people who were perceived as an inconvenience to their families and who might otherwise have been incarcerated with the genuinely insane.

The Act did not cover 'single lunatics', the most invisible of all mentally ill patients. Where just one lunatic was accommodated in a household, no licence was required to legally detain him or her; these types of patient were therefore extremely vulnerable to abuse.

More importantly, the new legislation did nothing to protect paupers, the patients who were most at risk from neglect or ill-treatment. As Andrew Scull explains in *The Most Solitary of Afflictions*, 'most proprietors of the institutions in which they were confined were attempting to extract a profit from the pittance which the parish overseers allowed for their maintenance.' The temptation to cut corners must have been very strong. The Act also did not apply to Bethlem or other charitable hospitals, or to workhouses and parish infirmaries.

One such instance of neglect in the York Lunatic Asylum led to the founding of another institution that would be hugely influential on the treatment of the mentally ill during the nineteenth century. In 1790, Hannah Mills, a Quaker, was admitted to the asylum in York suffering from 'melancholy'. Despite repeated attempts, local Quakers were refused admission to visit her. She died just a month later in squalid and inhumane conditions.

This shocked the Society of Friends, especially William Tuke, a prominent Quaker and retired tea merchant. He vowed that Quakers with a 'loss of reason' should never endure such suffering again. After deciding to build an asylum especially for them, Tuke garnered the Society of Friends' support.

The result was the purpose-built York Retreat, which opened in 1796. The conditions for patients were humane with minimal

The Retreat, York. (Wellcome Collection. CC BY)

physical restraint only used as a last resort; specifically, gyves (fetters or shackles), chains and manacles were done away with. The York Retreat sought to replicate a homely atmosphere, and the patients ate and worked with the staff. William Tuke's grandson Samuel wrote *Description of the Retreat* in 1813. In it, he explained, 'Neither chains nor corporal punishments are tolerated, on any pretext, in this establishment.' Violent patients 'require to be separated from the more tranquil, and to be prevented, by some means, from offensive conduct, towards their fellow-sufferers. Hence, the patients are arranged into classes, as much as they may be, according to the degree in which they approach to rational or orderly conduct.'

At a time when lunatics were routinely chained, this humane philosophy was markedly different. It became known as 'moral treatment' or 'moral therapy' and it was to greatly influence reformers of public lunatic asylums in the nineteenth century.

Case Study: Sarah Delves

Early records of lunatic asylums do not tend to provide as much detail about the treatment and daily lives of their patients as their Victorian counterparts. However, the registers for the York Retreat are one of the exceptions.

Sarah Delves née Summerland of Coalbrookdale, Shropshire was admitted to the asylum in November 1796 as case number fourteen. The Retreat had only opened in June that year and Sarah's admission was somewhat controversial because the asylum was exclusively for Quakers and she was classed as a non-member. She had 'married out' by marrying Joseph Delves, a non-Quaker, in 1764.

Sarah may have been accepted as a patient because her mother Ann Summerland was a prominent figure in the Coalbrookdale Quakers, having travelled up and down the country with Abiah Darby to spread the word. According to notes from a meeting of the Coalbrookdale Quakers in 1770, Sarah had also submitted a 'letter of condemnation' of her past conduct, asking to be re-admitted to the Society of Friends; this was accepted. It was the Coalbrookdale Quakers who paid for Sarah to be taken to the York Retreat on a horse and cart.

The Retreat admission register notes that Sarah had been a nurse and a servant before marrying and having a family. Her education and talents were described as 'defective' but her disposition was good. Her state of mind was 'mania & melancholy alternately'. The fee was four shillings per week and she had been sent by the North Wales Quarterly Meeting.

In her casebook notes, it was stated that she was about fifty-five and had been 'insane at times for 11 Years past, supposed to be occasion'd by unkind treatment from her Husband & untowardness of her children. She was at first very flighty and manifested an inclination to injure herself but grew better in about 3 Months and continued so for a few weeks; since that time she has had several short attacks of the disorder with long Intervals.' The casebook also notes that this was not Sarah's first time in an asylum as she had been confined at Bilson (probably the private madhouse at Bilston, Staffordshire) about a year previously and returned home well after three months, continuing so for some time.

The records also stated: 'She has frequently had a discharge of matter from her Ears, the Periods of which seem to alternate with her Fits of Insanity. Her Fits generally come on with lowness of spirits. When she is better she may safely be trusted to go at large in the House.'

A margin note added that Sarah 'Had been rather a giddy girl and had married imprudently out of the Society. She occasionally spoke in meetings when considered not in a sane state of mind, and was not a member of Society. She was a kind innocent and very inoffensive woman and was pitied and beloved by those who knew her best.'

On 20 November 1798, Sarah was discharged 'recovered' from the Retreat 'after a long trial' and returned home 'having been well a considerable time'. Sadly, she was not to enjoy her good health for long as she died at Coalbrookdale in 1799 'after slight relapses not requiring seclusion'.

Sources: The Retreat Admission Papers (RET 6/1/1a); Admission Register (RET 6/2/1/1) and Casebook (RET 6/5/1/1a); all at Borthwick Institute for Archives, University of York.

(With thanks to Sandra Halling (née Delves) for this information about her ancestor and to the Borthwick Institute for Archives, University of York for granting permission to quote from Sarah Delves' records.)

SCOTLAND AND IRELAND

Since the fourteenth century, Scottish law had made a distinction between the 'fatuous' (idiots and imbeciles) and the 'furious' (maniacs). Custody of those of 'furious mind' belonged to the Crown, it having the authority to coerce with fetters where necessary. Protection by the Crown was devolved to Chancery in a similar system to that of England and Wales.

Anyone wanting to declare their wealthy relative incapable of administering their affairs because of 'furiosity' or 'idiotry' could buy a brieve (a writ) from Chancery. A judge then held an inquest by jury to decide on the case. If the individual was found incapable, a curator was appointed to look after his or her affairs. From the eighteenth century, relatives could petition for a *'curator bonis'* at the Court of Session rather than the Sheriff Court.

Unlike England, Scotland did not have a tradition of institutional care for its lunatics. A few cities such as Edinburgh had a bedlam (established in 1698) whilst other lunatics might be accommodated in poorhouses or prisons, or boarded out with individuals. In 1781, the first charitable lunatic asylum was established in Montrose 'through the benevolence and indefatigable exertions of Mrs Susan Carnegie'. Previously, the insane of the town had been accommodated in the Old Tolbooth.

Almost twenty years later, in 1800, a small asylum with twelve cells was opened in Aberdeen, known as the Aberdeen Lunatic Hospital. This was built to replace cells for the insane that had been in existence at the Aberdeen Infirmary since the 1740s. Both institutions discovered that there was a high demand for places but only a small number of patients could be catered for.

In Ireland before 1800, there was some provision for lunatics at the houses of industry, founded in the towns and cities, for example, at Dublin from 1708. In addition, St Patrick's Hospital in Dublin had been funded by a bequest from the writer Jonathan Swift; until the nineteenth century, this was the only dedicated institution in Ireland for lunatics. There was just one private madhouse, opened at Cork in 1799, and at this time, the preference was still for out-relief and care in one's own home.

Chapter 2

LUNATIC ASYLUMS OF THE NINETEENTH CENTURY

> I believe there is hardly a parish of any considerable extent in which there may not be found some unfortunate creature of this description, who, if his ill treatment has made him phrenetic [*sic*], is chained in the cellar or garret of a workhouse, fastened to the leg of a table, tied to a post in an outhouse, or perhaps shut up in an uninhabited ruin … or if his lunacy be inoffensive, left to ramble half naked or half starved through the streets or highways, teased by the scoff and jest of all that is vulgar, ignorant and unfeeling.

So wrote Sir George Onesiphorus Paul, a Gloucestershire magistrate and philanthropist, to the Secretary of State about pauper lunatics in 1807. A Parliamentary Select Committee had been set up that year to enquire into the state of pauper and criminal lunatics in England and Wales, how many there were and where they were accommodated.

In 1800, there were about fifty private licensed madhouses in England, the majority of which accommodated both private and pauper patients. However, the lack of public asylums was becoming a source of national concern, as were the conditions and treatment in private madhouses.

The Parliamentary Select Committee found that under-reporting of lunatic pauper numbers was widespread. From the available documentation, it calculated that in England and Wales, there were 1,765 pauper lunatics in workhouses plus 483 in private custody, 113 in houses of correction and twenty-seven in gaols. It commented that 'these [figures] are so evidently deficient in several instances that a large addition must be made in any computation of the whole number.'

The Committee also discovered that Wales had no private madhouses or charitable asylums at all, continuing to prefer the system of 'farming out' instead of institutional care. Their findings led to the 1808 Act for the Better Care and Maintenance of Lunatics being passed the following year. This legislation allowed public money to be raised to build county lunatic asylums in England and Wales. Among the first to take advantage of the Act were Nottinghamshire, Bedfordshire, Lancashire, the West Riding of Yorkshire and Staffordshire. But the majority of counties were extremely reluctant to do so because of the considerable cost involved, and as the legislation was permissive, they continued to use private madhouses to accommodate their pauper lunatics. In fact, from 1808 to 1828, only ten such pauper lunatic asylums were established in England out of a total of fifty-two counties.

In 1814, scandals of mistreatment and neglect of pauper lunatics had been exposed at York Asylum by Yorkshire magistrate Godfrey Higgins and at Bethlem by Quaker Edward Wakefield. A number of government inquiries into charitable hospitals, county asylums, private madhouses and workhouses from 1815 to 1819 kept the issue of lunatics and their care firmly in the public spotlight.

Under-reporting of lunatics was a recurring theme. According to the official returns, in 1826, there were only about 1,600 in public asylums and fifty-three in gaols and houses of correction. Sir Andrew Halliday attributed the considerable discrepancies to 'the great irregularity and incorrectness of the returns made to Parliament'. For 1826, taking into account the large number of omitted counties, workhouses and asylums, he calculated there were actually 8,070 confined lunatics in England and Wales.

The 1774 Madhouses Act was strengthened by a series of laws passed from the 1820s, which established the Commissioners in Lunacy, first for London in 1828 and then for the rest of England and Wales in 1844. The Lunacy Commissioners were a permanent body of inspectors made up of doctors, lawyers and officials whose job it was to visit and report on asylums, without prior notice. They visited all premises housing lunatics including workhouses, registered hospitals and private madhouses. They had the power to prosecute and withdraw licences if inadequate care and treatment was not improved. The Commissioners ensured that the worst abuses were stamped out because proper keeping of patient records was required by law, as was the recording of all cases of physical restraint. Bethlem Hospital was excluded from the 1828 Act.

Much like failing schools, hospitals and businesses today, an asylum with a poor reputation could be 'turned around' by a new proprietor or medical superintendent. For example, in 1824, concerns were raised about how the charitable Newcastle Asylum was being run and the management was changed. Afterwards, the asylum was considerably enlarged and improved in terms of ventilation, classification and the comfort of the patients; numbers were restricted to eighty, rather than 100 as before.

When Dr Smith, the new medical superintendent, arrived at Newcastle in 1824, he discovered 'six miserable wretches … chained down in their melancholy cells'. They were all liberated and 'five of them now enjoy the liberties of their class, and, with others, amuse themselves in the large garden that belongs to the house. This affords a striking and convincing instance of the advantages derived from a soothing, kind and humane treatment of persons labouring under the most awful of all diseases.'

In 1827, it was stated that 'even the paupers are accommodated with warm, clean, separate beds, two or four in one room.' There were also airing yards, day rooms and a separate gallery, 'warmed by hot air from the fires and stoves below'. Each class had a water closet and all patients were well fed. The cost to parishes for boarding their pauper lunatics at the asylum was 9s 6d per week for males and 9s for females. Like many charitable asylums, Newcastle also took private patients to subsidise the paupers. These people, 'whose friends can pay for superior accommodation', had a 'neat bed-room and a sitting-room'.

PRIVATE ASYLUMS

In the 1830s and 1840s, the increasing number of lunatic patients put considerable pressure on Poor Law unions. The demand for asylum accommodation for those pauper lunatics who were too dangerous or too difficult to manage in workhouses was not met by the county asylums, of which there were an insufficient number at the time. As a result, charitable asylums and private madhouses continued to provide accommodation for lunatics, especially paupers. A number of new licensed private asylums were established to meet this demand, including Duddeston Hall Lunatic Asylum near Birmingham, opened in 1835.

From the early 1840s, private asylums were increasingly criticised by reformers who were particularly concerned about standards of care, the excessive use of mechanical restraint, and the poor accommodation for paupers. It was common for proprietors to buy an old mansion, use the impressive main building for the private patients and confine the paupers to the stables and outbuildings. This was the case at Duddeston Hall, which had previously been a banker's mansion. Run by surgeon Thomas Lewis, it was licensed for thirty private patients and sixty paupers. It was used by the Birmingham and Aston Poor Law unions, as well as Dudley, Kidderminster, Rugby, Nuneaton, Warwick and Solihull.

The difference between the living conditions and treatment for private patients and paupers at Duddeston was stark. L.D. Smith's article 'Duddeston Hall and the "Trade in Lunacy" 1835–1865' points out that the private patients 'were housed inside the mansion, with its spacious rooms' and 'allowed access to the gardens and grounds for recreation and exercise'. The wealthy convalescent patients were first to be let out of their rooms in the mornings and on Sunday evenings, 'they would be allowed the privilege of eating with the superintendent … and his family.'

By contrast, the paupers and the poorer private patients were accommodated in outbuildings 'which were of a much inferior standard'. Their beds were 'hard and knotty', with insufficient bedding. In a report by the Metropolitan Commissioners in Lunacy in 1844, it was noted that recreation for these patients consisted of 'one dull yard' each for the male and female paupers. Despite the poor living conditions, the Commissioners commented that Thomas Lewis treated the pauper patients with kindness.

Crucially, there was no set limit on the number of patients one keeper could be in charge of. Asylum proprietors could legally keep their costs low by employing few keepers, but to retain control and their own safety, those members of staff had to use mechanical restraint. For example, during the night at Duddeston, patients were locked in their rooms and the more disturbed and dangerous were strapped into their beds.

According to Andrew Scull, a staff to patient ratio of 1:10 or 1:12 was 'standard in the better county asylums' of the mid-nineteenth century. In private asylums, the number of attendants was much greater. The Lunacy Commissioners' Annual Report in 1847 noted that the ratio for 'high class patients' could be as high as one for every two patients. In *The Trade in Lunacy*, William Parry-Jones comments that in 1853 at Ticehurst, there were fifty-eight patients 'for whom, it was claimed, there were fifty-one attendants'. In the same year, 160 mostly pauper patients at Bensham Lunatic Asylum, Gateshead 'were cared for by only eleven attendants and at Fisherton House, the 214 patients were looked after by twenty-six attendants.'

It was difficult to attract and retain good quality staff for lunatic asylums until the end of the nineteenth century. Although the role of 'keeper' was renamed 'attendant' after 1845, there was no formal training, the pay was low and working conditions were poor. From

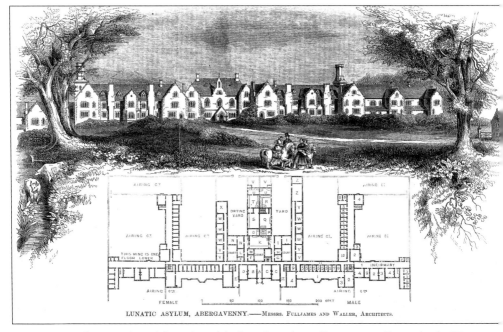

LUNATIC ASYLUM, ABERGAVENNY.——Messrs. Fulljames and Waller, Architects.

Facade, grounds and floor plan of the lunatic asylum, Abergavenny. Engraving by J.J. Laing after B. Sly after Fulljames and Waller. (Wellcome Collection. CC BY)

the 1890s, the term 'asylum nurse' was used to describe female attendants as nursing was beginning to develop as a profession.

COUNTY ASYLUMS

Public lunatic asylums were finally made compulsory in England and Wales after the Lunatic Asylum and Pauper Lunatics Act was passed in 1845 but, by then, two-thirds of county authorities had already provided asylums for the mentally ill. Under the terms of the Act, all counties and boroughs were compelled by law to establish publicly funded asylums to house pauper lunatics within three years. By 1850, there were twenty-four county and borough asylums in England and Wales, with accommodation for an average of just under 300 lunatics in each.

In 1844, there was still no public lunatic asylum in Wales for the 1,177 pauper lunatics living there. Haverfordwest in Pembrokeshire had appropriated the town jail for pauper lunatics in 1822 and called it a 'county asylum'. However, as Andrew Roberts points out in his index of English and Welsh lunatic asylums (http://studymore. org.uk/4_13_ta.htm#Wales), no alterations or extensions were made to the building and there was just a keeper and his wife to look after the patients, so it was not a 'proper' asylum.

Welsh Poor Law unions continued to use private asylums to house their pauper lunatics. For example, Vernon House Asylum at Briton Ferry near Swansea was a private institution licensed to take both pauper and private patients. However, in 1858, there were 183 paupers and only twenty-six private patients.

In Wales, it was necessary for counties to join together and form unions to build 'joint asylums'. The first public asylum for Welsh lunatics was actually in England: the Shropshire Asylum, opened in 1845. The following year, it became the Shropshire and Montgomeryshire Counties and Wenlock Borough County Asylum.

The first public asylum to be built in Wales opened in 1848 at Denbigh as the North Wales County Asylum; it served the counties of Flint, Denbigh, Merioneth, Caernarvon and Anglesey. In 1851, the counties of Monmouthshire, Herefordshire, Breconshire, Radnorshire and the City of Hereford established the Joint Counties Asylum at Abergavenny. The Glamorgan County Lunatic Asylum at Angelton near Bridgend finally opened in 1864, followed a year later by the United Lunatic Asylum for Carmarthenshire, Cardigan and Pembrokeshire.

Poor Law unions still used private madhouses for 'overflow' paupers, especially in populous areas where the new county asylums were quickly filled up. There was a lucrative market for private madhouses to accommodate pauper lunatics, particularly in areas that had not yet opened a county or borough asylum.

Parishes and Poor Law unions needed to keep their costs down to reduce the burden on their ratepayers. They therefore frequently 'shopped around' to find the lowest prices for asylum care; this led many private madhouses to undercut their rivals in the same locality in order to retain contracts or be awarded new ones.

Whenever a public asylum was founded in a particular area, there was a huge impact on the private institutions serving that county because a large proportion of their income disappeared overnight along with the departing paupers.

In August 1852, when Worcester County Lunatic Asylum first opened at Powick, the guardians of the Dudley Union Workhouse immediately transferred their pauper lunatics from three private madhouses to the new institution; the minutes of the Board of Guardians record that twelve were removed from Droitwich Asylum, six from Duddeston Hall and three from Hunningham House, Warwickshire. A year earlier, the guardians had transferred six inmates from private madhouses to Staffordshire Lunatic Asylum when vacancies had occurred. The inference is clear: it was cheaper to accommodate pauper lunatics in a county asylum rather than a private institution. William Parry Jones notes that 'by 1843, the average weekly cost for the maintenance, clothing and treatment of English pauper lunatics in private licensed houses was 8s 11½d, compared with 7s 6¾d in the county asylums.'

Private asylums that chose not to take paupers were marketed as being more comfortable than the county asylums. In an advertisement for Ashwood House in Kingswinford, Staffordshire from around 1879, the proprietor and medical superintendent George Fowler Bodington described the rooms in his asylum as 'large, lofty and cheerful'. The house, both inside and outside, had 'entirely the air and character of a gentleman's private residence'. The patients associated with the proprietor's family and 'every possible freedom' was allowed them 'consistent with safety'. Carriage exercise was provided, as well as books, newspapers and magazines; in addition, there was a billiard room, a large croquet lawn and about 40 acres of gardens and grounds. The patients were also 'entertained with music and a variety of other means of

ASHWOOD HOUSE,

KINGSWINFORD, STAFFORDSHIRE.

A Private Asylum for Ladies and Gentlemen.

GEORGE FOWLER BODINGTON, M.D., M.R.C.P., F.R.C.S. (Exam.)

Proprietor and Medical Superintendent.

Ashwood House is a large mansion in the county of Stafford, close upon the borders of Worcestershire. It is very substantially built, and is situated upon an elevated spot commanding extensive views. The rooms are large, lofty, and cheerful, and the house, both inside and outside, has entirely the air and character of a gentleman's private residence. The soil is sand and gravel, has excellent natural drainage, and is very dry. The gardens and grounds, about forty acres in extent, are well planted with shrubs and ornamental timber, and are extremely picturesque. The climate is genial, and the locality notoriously healthy. The country around is secluded and quiet, and affords a great variety of walks and drives amidst the most charming scenery.

The patients associate with the Proprietor's family, and have every possible freedom allowed them consistent with safety.

Carriage exercise is provided; there is a Billiard Room, and a large Croquet Lawn; Books, Newspapers, and Magazines are supplied, and the patients are entertained with music and a variety of other means of recreation and amusement.

Divine service is held in the House every Sunday afternoon.

This establishment has lately been removed from Driffold House, Sutton Coldfield, Warwickshire, where it was carried on for thirty-six years by Dr. Bodington and his father. The following extract is from the Report of the Lunacy Commissioners [July, 1872]:—

"Driffold House, Sutton Coldfield, near Birmingham, is now very judiciously managed, and uniformly satisfactory account has been given lately of the accommodation and the treatment of its patients of both sexes . . . . all of them receiving much attention and kindness from Dr. Bodington's family."—*26th Annual Report of the Commissioners in Lunacy,* p. 44.

STOURBRIDGE and DUDLEY are the nearest railway stations. Postal Address—

DR. BODINGTON,

ASHWOOD HOUSE,

KINGSWINFORD,

STAFFORDSHIRE.

4 R 2   1363

Advertising leaflet for Ashwood House, circa 1879. (Wellcome Collection. CC BY) recreation and amusement'. Divine service was held in the house every Sunday afternoon. By 1881, there were twenty-five patients, with one matron and eight attendants.

After the scandals of the early nineteenth century, Bethlem continued in its role as a charitable lunatic asylum. In 1815, it moved to a new site in St George's Fields, Southwark, where there were extensive grounds for recreation and exercise. The building could accommodate 198 patients and there was plenty of space for expansion when needed. A new wing was begun in the 1830s for an additional 166 patients; there were also two wings specifically for criminal lunatics. The building comprised four storeys with a central block flanked by two wings, one for males and one for females.

Bethlem was excluded from the Metropolitan Commissioners in Lunacy's regular inspections but in 1844, they noted that there were 355 patients, of whom ninety were criminals. Six years later, the Commissioners obtained a Secretary of State's warrant to inspect Bethlem following allegations of ill-treatment by attendants. The resulting report was critical and subsequently, the new medical superintendent William Hood's 'humane and enlightened principles' were the basis of all treatments. In 1853, Bethlem became a Registered Hospital with the Lunacy Commission and was regularly inspected. After 1857, Bethlem no longer accepted pauper patients, instead focusing on the educated working and middle classes 'in a presumably curable condition'.

As noted in *Old and New London*, Bethlem did not accept patients who were 'proper object[s] for admission into a pauper county asylum', those who could afford to pay for treatment in a private asylum, those who had been insane for more than a year and considered incurable by the Bethlem physician, those who were idiots or subject to epileptic fits or 'whose condition threatens the speedy dissolution of life, or require the permanent and exclusive attendance of a nurse'. With these strict rules on admission, particularly excluding the incurable, Bethlem did not become overcrowded like the county asylums.

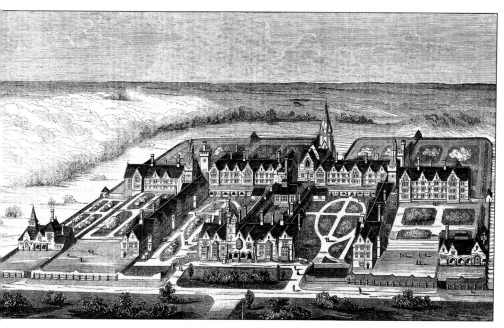

The County Lunatic Asylum, Brentwood, Essex: bird's-eye view. Wood engraving by W.E. Hodgkin, 1857, after H.E. Kendall. (Wellcome Collection. CC BY)

Case Study: Charles Rust

Although many people were long-stay patients in lunatic asylums, others were repeatedly discharged 'recovered' or 'cured' and had periods of good health before being readmitted at regular intervals.

Born in 1799 in Wethersfield, Essex, Charles Rust worked as an agricultural labourer. He married Jane Shelford in 1824 and by 1841, they had five children listed on the census.

The Lunacy Patients' Admission Registers reveal that Charles was admitted to Hoxton Asylum in Shoreditch, Middlesex on 18 January 1851 and discharged 'cured' a few months later on 23 April; the cause for his admission is not known. This must have been a very difficult time for Charles's wife. Two of her sons had already left home but she had had two more children since the previous census. No occupation is recorded for her on the 1851 census but she had five sons to look after. Two were old enough at twenty-six and seventeen to be bringing in an adult wage; the next two were eleven and nine and already working as 'farmer's boys'. The youngest son was just three years old.

On 22 March 1854, Charles was admitted to Essex County Asylum at Warley, Brentwood for the first time. The supposed cause was 'grief through loss of work' and he was suspected of being suicidal. He had been refusing to get out of bed or to eat for three days. The county asylum had opened the previous year so the majority of Essex patients would have been sent there, rather than Hoxton. Often, a period of time away from the stresses of daily life together with a nutritious diet could radically improve a person's mental health. This seems to have been the case for Charles, who was discharged 'cured' on 25 August that year.

A couple of years passed before Charles was readmitted to the Essex County Asylum on 8 November 1856. The supposed cause was that for the previous six weeks, Charles had been unable to work and he had inflammation in his eye. By now, he was described as 'very much depressed and highly suicidal' and was 'in very feeble health from refusal of food'. Again, Charles was discharged 'cured' on 6 June 1857.

On 9 March 1859, Charles was admitted again to Essex County Asylum. As before, he was in a very weak state of health and 'much depressed and suicidal'. The supposed cause now was 'intemperance' for the previous four months. The physician recorded that Charles had been unwilling to take his food, was disinclined to be seen, inattentive to his person and suffering from general despondency. Charles's wife also stated that 'he left his bed this morning & returned after immersing himself in the river.' Despite this suicide attempt and his poor health, Charles was well enough to be discharged 'cured' just a few months later, on 23 June.

Two years later, Charles had a longer stay at the Essex County Asylum from 19 November 1861 to 7 June 1862 due to 'want of employment'. This time, the Notice of Admission stated that Charles 'thinks his soul is lost, that he has no hope of mercy' and that he was in a very weak state of health. The physician noted on the medical certificate Charles's 'refusal to take food, fancying he cannot swallow' and his 'disregard to personal cleanliness & disinclination to be seen'. His wife added that he was noisy and restless at night. Luckily for her, the three remaining children at home were all of working age so they could contribute to the household income while Charles was being treated.

Charles's final stay at the Essex County Asylum began on 14 September 1865. The Notice of Admission states that Charles was 'very depressed, thinks his soul is lost & he refuses food'; as a result, he was in a very weak state of health. The supposed cause was illness of his wife and the physician noted Charles's general despondency. Four months later, his wife Jane died. This may have been the final straw for Charles as there was to be no short stay at the asylum this time. His physical health must have improved but he remained there until his death on 30 January 1879, aged eighty-three, and was interred in the asylum's burial ground.

Sources: Lunacy Patients' Admission Registers; at The National Archives and digitised on Ancestry (www.ancestry.co. uk).

Essex County Lunatic Asylum Patient Reception Orders (A/H 10/2/11/1/6 admission number 327; A/H 10/2/11/1/13 admission number 668; A/H 10/2/11/1/18 admission number 967; A/H 10/2/11/2/7 admission number 1374; and A/H 10/2/11/2/17 admission number 1958); all at Essex Record Office.

(With thanks to Trevor Beal for this information about his three times great-grandfather and to Essex Record Office for permission to quote from Charles Rust's records.)

RISING PATIENT NUMBERS

In 1844, the Lunacy Commissioners had stressed that the objective of county asylums 'is, or ought to be, the cure of insanity'; they were not designed to simply incarcerate patients. Acute cases, in which the illness had not manifested itself for long, were deemed to be curable and there was a good chance of recovery. Time away from the stresses of daily life with fresh air, work therapy and nutritious food could significantly improve a person's mental well-being.

However, asylum patient numbers in England and Wales increased relentlessly from 12,000 in 1850 to 27,000 in 1870. The wards filled up with chronic cases and fewer and fewer patients were being discharged; these included senile and demented people, those with epilepsy and general paralysis of the insane, as well as those with other neurological disorders. Magistrates were also being encouraged to send difficult, recurrent offenders from the workhouse or jail to an asylum. By 1860, county asylums housing from 500 to 800 patients were common. With such large numbers in so-called 'lunatic colonies', it was simply impossible to provide individual treatment. In London and Lancashire, asylums were built to cater for more than 2,000 patients.

For the senile elderly, an institution for lunatics could easily become their last home. In its annual report of 1875, the administrators of the Somerset County Pauper Lunatic Asylum argued that 'It is cruel to send persons whose insanity is nothing but the natural decay of age, to die in the Asylum.' In that year, patients had been admitted 'at the patriarchal ages of 83, 88 and 94 years of age, some certified even in this their day of dotage, as "dangerous to others"'.

The increase in patient numbers nationally put severe pressure on the asylums and many had to extend their accommodation to cope. In Wales, the Abergavenny Asylum was extended between 1857 and 1859 to provide beds for 466 patients. Another extension built between 1873 and 1875 provided seventy more beds but the demand continued and 250 extra places were created in 1881.

Another option was for Poor Law unions to send paupers to a less overcrowded asylum outside the county. This resulted in patients being frequently moved between institutions, regardless of the effect such a major change might have on them or whether relatives would find it more difficult to visit an asylum further away. There was also an additional cost for Poor Law unions. In 1849, the Surrey County Lunatic Asylum charged those within Surrey nine shillings weekly for the maintenance of their pauper lunatics; the cost for paupers from outside the county was fourteen shillings per week.

By 1890, there were sixty-six county asylums in England and Wales that could accommodate an average of more than 800 lunatics per institution. In that year, a consolidating Act was passed requiring two medical certificates for all lunatic patients, including paupers. This was designed to strengthen the safeguards against improper confinement of sane people. Before, private patients had not needed an order from a Justice of the Peace prior to admission but now a 'reception order' was required for all types of patients, except Chancery lunatics.

Under the legislation, county and borough asylums could also build separate buildings or wards for private patients furnished and decorated to standards to which the upper and upper middle classes were accustomed. Pauper lunatics could also be 'absent on trial' and boarded out with friends or relatives; they would receive an allowance, which was not to exceed the amount the asylum would have charged for in-patient care.

After 1890, an increasing number of patients in private asylums were voluntary 'boarders' who were not certified. They had chosen to seek treatment and could leave after giving twenty-four hours' notice.

In *Medical Services and the Hospitals of Britain*, Steven Cherry points out that the new legislation coincided with certain measures designed to 'reduce the stigma surrounding mental illness'. This included early outpatient clinics such as the one at Wakefield in early 1890 and in the other West Riding Asylums, the development of reception and observation wards in some asylums and the setting up of the first psychiatric units in some Scottish hospitals.

By 1900, there were over 100,000 inmates in English and Welsh asylums, with others housed in workhouses or in licensed houses. In Scotland, the number of asylum patients increased from 6,000 in 1860 to 16,700 in 1914. Lunatic asylums were now places where chronic, incurable patients with no hope of recovery were confined.

Case Study: Emily Thomas
Today, if a mother was experiencing hallucinations and delusions after childbirth, she would probably be diagnosed with postpartum psychosis. She would receive specialist care and support in hospital, often in a mother and baby unit, and be offered antipsychotic drugs and antidepressants. Sadly, such care was not available to Victorian mothers with the same symptoms; instead, they were incarcerated in an asylum and separated from their children. Only on rare occasions when patients had clearly recovered were they allowed to go home and resume their lives.

This was not to happen in the case of Emily Thomas (née Cole), who was admitted to Hanwell, the Middlesex County Lunatic Asylum, on 18 September 1863. Born in Chelsea in 1832, she had married George Thomas, a Thames waterman like her father, in 1851. They had four children in quick succession between 1858 and May 1863: Emily, William, Louisa and George. Baby George was born four months before Emily was certified with mental illness. It's not known if there were any previous pregnancies resulting in miscarriages, still births or deaths in infancy.

In any case, in 1863, Emily had three children under the age of five to look after, plus a four-month-old baby, and it became very clear that she was unable to cope. Her mental illness had first started three months earlier and her medical certificate stated she was 'irrational on almost every subject, imagines herself unable to do any household work, cannot wash her children or clean her house'. Emily was certified as being 'dangerous to others' because she had 'threatened the lives of her children and husband'.

On admission to Hanwell, Emily was diagnosed with melancholia. Three days later, her husband George provided more information about her case. After baby George's birth four months earlier, Emily got up after five weeks (the traditional lying-in period could range from two weeks to two months, depending on the mother's social class and health). Emily began to have 'apprehensions of various kinds' and said the children were going to die. She had been low and depressed while pregnant because she lost her sister-in-law in confinement and thought the same thing would happen to her. On being advised to go into the country, Emily became noisy and threatening, and she imagined there was 'a little black fellow to take her away crouched in the corner'.

She then took to screaming and would scream for ten minutes, and often for a quarter of an hour. At about the same time, Emily accused her friends of wishing to poison her and refused to eat anything, so she had to be fed. She had never been violent or destructive before but she 'frequently threatened her husband with [a] knife' and 'threatened several times to destroy the Children. Said they were not wanted here "that she should chuck them into the River".'

The medical officer at Hanwell did attribute Emily's mental illness to 'puerperium' (the period of around six weeks after childbirth), but he also believed that heredity played a part. Her husband stated that two of Emily's female cousins had 'at the ages 23 and 24, destroyed themselves. One took poison & the other drowned herself.' The 'Loss of Relative by death in Confinement while pregnant' also contributed to Emily's mental breakdown, and her illness meant she was destined to spend the rest of her life in the asylum and be kept apart from her children.

Emily's asylum records are typical of many long-stay Victorian patients in that they are not very detailed; in fact, there is rarely more than one entry per year. In 1864, the year after her admission, the only entry reads, 'no decided improvement in this case'. Emily worked in the Officers' Laundry and was 'very industrious' but she was also troublesome, excitable and violent at times. In July 1867, she threatened to throw a hot iron at another patient.

Five years later, there was no mental improvement and Emily was still experiencing delusions of sight and hearing, but she continued to be industrious. In 1878, the medical officer wrote that Emily had delusions about her husband and that she 'fancies he has given her the "bad disorder"'. Emily's husband George had, in fact, died six years earlier of apoplexy and their children were being looked after by various members of the family.

In February 1880, more details were added about Emily's state of mind. She was 'usually grumbling about her detention here & is prone to excitement'. It appears that her delusions had developed because she had 'a high notion of her own importance; talks about the money she possesses & imagines that most of the former Assistant Medical Officers are now in Newgate Gaol by her orders. Says that people beneath her bed disturb her stomach & "jaunt her" at night; they are first men & then change into women.' Emily was still an industrious worker in the Officers' Laundry but 'quarrelsome'.

By November 1881, Emily believed 'her friends are in different parts of the house waiting to take her out. Says she can hear them calling her.' She also accused 'several patients of going out and meeting her husband' and threatened to 'smash their heads with a flat-iron'.

In July 1890, Emily's delusions continued unabated but started to focus more specifically on her family. She called the nurses and other patients her daughters and said that 'her father and brothers were in the building, that she has the freedom of the City, that she owns a large number of barges'. By October, she commented that her husband was dead but 'she believes he is here with a lot of other dead people'. In January 1892, Emily said that she was twenty-one years old and that 'her son William is concealed in the building & they won't let him come to her.' By 1895, Emily was still 'full of delusions concerning invisibles'.

Five years later, Emily became ill with a heart condition and died on 18 June 1900 aged sixty-eight. She had spent thirty-seven years at Hanwell. Her four children lived well into the twentieth century without any mental health problems.

Sources: Hanwell Asylum Register of Admissions (H11/HLL/B/05/005); Casebook for Female Patients (H11/HLL/B/19/012); Continuation Casebook (H11/HLL/B19/064); Register of Female Deaths (H11/HLL/B/15/003); all at London Metropolitan Archives, City of London.

(With thanks to Maureen Long for this information about her great-great-grandmother, and to West London NHS Trust for permission to quote from Emily Thomas's records.)

ASYLUMS IN SCOTLAND

Under new legislation introduced in 1815, 1828 and 1841, attempts were made to regulate the confinement and treatment of Scottish pauper lunatics. In particular, the 1815 Act to Regulate Madhouses in Scotland made sheriffs responsible for licensing and inspecting private asylums and madhouses in their districts. Licences were renewed annually and the sheriffs made inspections twice a year. They also issued warrants to commit pauper lunatics to asylums and liberated anyone who was illegally detained as a lunatic. After the Madhouses Amendment (Scotland) Act of 1828, it was compulsory to have a warrant from a sheriff before the admission or discharge of a patient could take place. If an asylum or madhouse accommodated more than 100 people, a medical practitioner was required to visit twice a week. Proper admission and discharge records had to be kept and presented for inspection by sheriffs and Justices of the Peace.

In the early nineteenth century, five more charitable asylums were established in the main urban centres of Scotland. Edinburgh

Lunatic Asylum at Morningside was opened in 1813 after being granted a royal charter. At first, it was only for private patients but in 1842, a new building was added to accept paupers. Two years later, patients from the Edinburgh bedlam were transferred to the asylum.

The Glasgow Asylum for Lunatics opened in 1814, becoming a royal asylum in 1824. The original building was built to the radial design based on Jeremy Bentham's panopticon theory to provide optimum supervision and security. A new asylum was built at Gartnavel in 1843. After 1889, Gartnavel no longer accepted pauper lunatics and instead developed into one of Britain's foremost fee-paying psychiatric hospitals.

There were changes too at the oldest charitable asylums in Montrose and Aberdeen. Montrose was granted a royal charter in 1810 and a new building with improved facilities and accommodation was completed in 1858 on farmland at Sunnyside, outside Montrose.

A new asylum was also opened in Aberdeen in 1820; two years earlier, the total number of patients had reached sixty-three. The new building could accommodate another 150 patients. By 1857, the average daily number of patients was 291. The superintendent's house, built in 1852 and known as Clerkseat House, was also used as overflow accommodation. In the same year, the institution became known as Aberdeen Royal Lunatic Asylum. Elmhill House was built on the adjoining estate and opened in 1862, especially for private patients who could pay a guinea or more per week. Surrounded by an extensive park and pleasure grounds, it was designed to accommodate sixty-five ladies and gentlemen in 'the maximum of comfort'. The house was not suitable for acute or troublesome cases, and these would be transferred, often temporarily, to the main asylum. The Glack estate in the parish of Daviot was purchased in 1888 to serve as an extension to the main asylum and to offer farm work to the patients who came from rural areas.

Opened in 1820, Dundee Royal Lunatic Asylum was linked with

the Dundee Royal Infirmary. The asylum was founded 'to restore the use of reason, to alleviate suffering and to lessen peril where reason cannot be restored'. Its royal charter had been granted the year before and at first, there were just fifty patients. The number increased to 105 by 1828, and to 200 by 1839.

The Murray Royal Lunatic Asylum in Perth was opened in 1827. It was founded by James Murray, who died in 1814 leaving two-thirds of his estate to establish an asylum in the Perth area. Originally, there was accommodation for eighty patients but the building was extended in 1833. In addition, a villa nearby was bought in 1848 specifically for the 'higher class' patients.

Crichton Institution for Lunatics was founded in 1838 and opened a year later. It was endowed by Dr James Crichton, and his widow Elizabeth sought to use the funds for 'founding and endowing a lunatic asylum in the neighbourhood of Dumfries'. Crichton was granted a royal charter in 1840 and had accommodation for 120 pauper and private patients.

The Crichton Royal Institution, Dumfries, Scotland. Transfer lithograph by Fr. Schenck. (Wellcome Collection. CC BY)

In 1828, Sir Andrew Halliday estimated there were about 3,700 lunatics and idiots in Scotland: 643 of these were in private or public asylums, workhouses or the bedlam at Edinburgh; 1,192 were 'confined with private individuals, principally with small farmers and cottagers'; and twenty-one were in gaols. This made a total of 1,861 in confinement whilst upwards of 1,600 'are allowed to be at large, most of them wandering over the country, and subsisting by begging'. Nearly half of the insane or 1,634 were maintained by the public.

The only asylum in Scotland built specifically for paupers before 1857 was the Elgin Pauper Lunatic Asylum, which opened in 1835. Despite the campaigning of Halliday and others to highlight the inadequacies of the Scottish asylum system, it was the work of Dorothea Dix, an American asylum reformer, that forced a royal commission to examine the issue. She visited Scotland in 1855 and discovered poor living conditions and inhumane treatment in the asylums, madhouses and homes.

In the same year, the Royal Commission on Lunacy in Scotland found evidence of neglect and ill-treatment of lunatic patients, as well as profiteering in the private homes. All types of accommodation were criticised for their methods of trussing and restraint, especially during the transport of patients to asylums, which could cause physical injury.

The Royal Commission estimated there were 4,800 lunatics and 2,600 congenital idiots in Scotland. To cater for this number of mentally afflicted, there were the seven royal chartered asylums, the public asylum at Elgin, twenty-three private licensed madhouses, seventeen poorhouses with separate wards for lunatics, additional poorhouses without separate wards, the lunatic department of the General Prison in Perth, private houses reported to the sherriff, private houses of relatives and strangers not reported.

The report of the Royal Commission concluded, 'there can be no doubt that the public accommodation provided for the insane in Scotland is insufficient to meet the needs of the community.' As a result, the 1857 Lunacy (Scotland) Act was passed; under this legislation, new district asylums were built, which were state run, as part of the Poor Law, and administered by the parish. The first was the asylum for Argyll and Bute, which opened in 1863, and by 1910, a further eighteen such asylums had been built. The Scottish legislation was deemed more liberal than in England and Wales because it allowed for voluntary admission to asylums and for the boarding out of lunatics in the community. When Christian Watt, a widowed fishwife, was first admitted to the Aberdeen Royal Lunatic Asylum, and on two subsequent stays, she went as a voluntary patient for a 'rest', as recommended by her doctor. She was not certified as insane until she had had a complete mental breakdown in 1879, as described in her memoirs, *The Christian Watt Papers*.

THE IRISH ASYLUM SYSTEM

Perhaps surprisingly, Ireland was the first country in Europe to have a public lunatic asylum system, long before it was made compulsory in England and Wales. This was despite the fact there was no formal Poor Law in Ireland until 1838, when the English Poor Laws were introduced.

In 1815, the Richmond Lunatic Asylum in Dublin was opened, which was separate from the Dublin House of Industry and was highly regarded for its moral treatment.

The Select Committee on Lunatic Poor in Ireland of 1817 had found disturbing conditions in prisons and houses of industry where lunatics were usually accommodated. It recommended that a network of public district lunatic asylums be established on the Richmond model. The 1821 Irish Lunatic Asylums for the Poor Act was subsequently passed. From 1825 to 1835, nine district lunatic asylums were established at Armagh, Limerick, Belfast, Londonderry, Carlow, Connacht, Maryborough, Clonmel and Waterford. The Richmond Asylum in Dublin and the Cork Asylum later became district lunatic asylums and a criminal lunatic asylum opened at Dundrum in 1850. Further public lunatic asylums followed later in the century, with twelve more built from 1852 to 1869.

Under the Irish system, an insane person could be admitted to an asylum if a member of his or her family requested admission. They could also be incarcerated under the Dangerous Lunatics Act, passed in 1838. Anyone behaving in a manner believed to be insane or dangerous could be taken before two Justices of the Peace and examined by a medical practitioner. If declared insane, he or she would be committed to an asylum under the Lord Lieutenant's warrant; no other witness statements or proof were required.

From 1820 to 1870, the number of private madhouses in Ireland grew from six to twenty, and more than half were located in County Dublin. There was just one such institution in Northern Ireland in 1921: the Quaker Retreat at Armagh, opened in 1827.

By 1851, there were 3,234 patients being treated in Irish lunatic asylums; this rose to 16,941 by 1914. Ireland now had one of the world's largest growth of admissions into asylums per head of population.

Chapter 3

TWENTIETH-CENTURY MENTAL INSTITUTIONS

When a journalist for the periodical *Living London* visited Bethlem in 1902, he described it as 'the centre whence the latest knowledge pertaining to the medical aspects of lunacy are diffused all over the world'. In the extensive grounds, there was 'life and movement, and the babble of voices and the sound of joyous laughter'. There was an all-the-year-round cricket ground and seven or eight tennis courts on which some of the male patients were playing: 'Not at all like prisoners are those men. And, indeed, some of them are not such in any sense whatever. Several could walk into Lambeth Road this minute, for they are voluntary boarders – patients, that is to say, who have come here of their own free will and without being certified.'

Inside, in one of the female wards, there was a 'bright and cheerful air and a dominating note of comfort. Some of the female patients are occupied with needlework; in the middle distance a young lady is seated at one of the many excellent pianos that are scattered about the building; and beyond her another female guest is working and curing herself simultaneously by painting flowers on the panels of the door leading to the adjoining ward. The pursuit of art, as well as of music, and literature, is encouraged to the utmost.'

Bethlem's policy of not accepting incurable patients remained unchanged until 1948, so the institution did not suffer from overcrowding; in 1902, it was completely full and admissions were halted. However, people with general paralysis of the insane were

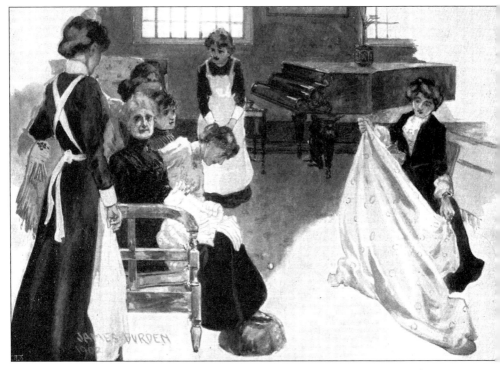

'Needlework at Bethlem' in 'Lunatic London'. (From Living London, *1902)*

admitted to Bethlem and this condition almost always led to the patient's death. Bethlem moved to its current site in Beckenham, Kent in 1930.

Sadly, Bethlem's 'bright and cheerful air' was the exception to the rule in Edwardian lunatic asylums in England. Generally, they were overcrowded, understaffed and underfunded, with thousands of patients being treated in each institution. Following the Lunacy Act of 1890, 'voluntary boarders' could be admitted to lunatic asylums. From 1900 to 1916, there was a marked rise in these types of patients, with a fall in certified ones.

In 1903, Croydon's newly built institution was the first in England to have the title of 'mental hospital' instead of 'lunatic asylum'. This reflected a desire to reduce the stigma of mental illness and a shift towards viewing it as a disease just like physical illnesses. The Lunacy Commission itself became the Board of Control in 1913. After the First World War, many asylums started to describe themselves as mental hospitals but it was not until the Mental Treatment Act of 1930 that all lunatic asylums in England and Wales were renamed mental hospitals. The word 'mental' was removed after the Second World War.

In early twentieth-century Scotland, the number of mental patients in institutions was half that of England, mostly because of the boarding out of harmless lunatics in private houses. In addition, pioneering wards for observation and treatment of mentally ill patients were being set up in the poorhouse system. A small ward with six beds for each gender was established at Barnhill Poorhouse as early as 1890. This led to other Scottish parish councils doing the same. In 1906, Glasgow Parish Council provided twenty-five-bed wards for each gender at the parochial hospital in Duke Street; parish councils of Dundee, Govan and Paisley also followed suit.

Large-scale institutions for the mentally ill did not appear in Wales until the early twentieth century as the Welsh still favoured boarding out, usually on farms. Outdoor relief was cheaper than asylum care and arguably better psychologically for patients than becoming institutionalised.

Case Study: Mary Ann Willis

The inability to cope with the death of a loved one could easily cause a person to have a mental breakdown. Born in Waltham Abbey in 1853, Mary Ann Chapman was the daughter of a farmer and one of thirteen children. In 1872, she married George Willis of Epping and they set up home above the butcher's shop in the High Street, where George had a business; Mary Ann kept the account books for her husband. She and George went on to have eight children, all but one surviving to adulthood.

*Mary Ann Willis with her husband George and six of their children, circa 1897.
(With thanks to Pam Chapman)*

By the 1891 census, there was a change in occupation for George as the couple were running the Crown Hotel at Loughton, Essex. This move into hospitality must have been successful because in 1897, they took over the tenancy of the Saracen's Head Inn and Hotel in Great Dunmow. Sadly, just a year later, tragedy struck when George died of liver failure, probably as a result of haemochromatosis, aged just forty-eight.

Mary Ann was left to run the business, probably with the help of her sons and second eldest daughter, Ethel Mary, who had started training as a nurse but returned home to assist her mother. Over the next few years, the family unit gradually reduced in size. In 1899, two of Mary Ann's daughters, Minnie Gertrude and Annie Caroline, got married in a double wedding. This was no doubt a bittersweet occasion for Mary Ann, but worse was to follow. In August 1900, the whole family was devastated when Annie Caroline died, leaving a baby son; this hit Mary Ann hard. In the same year, eldest son George Chapman Willis left to fight in the Boer War; two more sons followed in 1901 and 1902. They eventually returned home safely but the worry about them fighting so far away took its toll on Mary Ann.

It must have seemed as though the help she could rely on from her family to run the hotel was being withdrawn, bit by bit. On the 1901 census, there were just three members of live-in staff to help her: a barmaid, a waitress and a housemaid. The combination of grief over losing her husband and daughter, and the stress and worry about the business all became too much until she could no longer cope with daily life.

Mary Ann was admitted to Bethlem on 16 April 1902 as a private patient, at the request of her eldest son, who had returned from the Boer War. Her symptoms of mental illness had begun three months earlier and the casebook notes reveal the family had tried to solve the problem by employing two nurses to look after her at home for the previous month. However, she 'slept and took her food badly' and 'had the idea her children were all being murdered & that the room was full of electricity'. In addition, she 'did not recognise those outside the family', for example, her doctor, whom she knew well. She also 'imagined business was going to the bad', believing that the hotel licence would be taken away, which was not the case.

At Bethlem, Mary Ann was diagnosed with melancholia attributed to 'business worries'. Interestingly, grief was not mentioned, although it would undoubtedly have been a contributory factor. On admission, she was described as looking 'somewhat older than her years'. She was 'suspicious and taciturn and when she can be got to speak it is only in short sentences, and she complains that she should not be here.' Although she was clean in her habits, she was 'somewhat restless'. By 30 April, she was rather less restless, probably because she had been prescribed paraldehyde (a sedative). However, she thought her food was poisoned.

A week later, her mental condition was unchanged and she was 'still in a padded room in strong clothes'. No explanation for this is given in the records, although Mary Ann had been agitated in bed. As the months went by, she continued to be restless, depressed, and 'troublesome with food'. In July, it was noted that because of her deep-seated suspicion about her food she 'had to be fed on one or two occasions'. It's likely that this simply meant she was spoon-fed; there is no note of 'fed by tube' in Mary Ann's records as there would normally be if she had been fed in this manner.

In April 1903, a year after being first admitted, she was described as 'a case of chronic agitated melancholia with dementia'. On 8 July that year, she was discharged 'uncured' and transferred to the Essex County Lunatic Asylum at Brentwood, where she stayed for a short period. She was discharged to her brother's house in Waltham Abbey but by May 1904, her health had deteriorated and she was admitted to the City of London Asylum at Stone in Dartford, Kent as a private patient.

At this point, it's likely that Mary Ann's family knew she would never recover and tried to get on with their lives. Ethel Mary resumed her training as a nurse, qualifying in 1909. Three of Mary Ann's sons emigrated to Canada, New Zealand and Australia between 1908 and 1910, never to return, while another died suddenly in 1913. It's not known if Mary Ann's daughters ever visited her in any of the asylums she was treated in, but her mental illness was a well-kept family secret to later generations, only divulged in hushed tones.

Mary Ann was to spend the last decade of her life in the City of London Asylum, dying in November 1914 of an abscess in her jaw and bronchopneumonia. She was buried at St Mary's Church, Dunmow, in the same grave as her husband George.

Sources: Bethlem General Admission Register (ARA-39-254 and ARA-39-255), Bethlem Patient Casebooks (CB-168-258 and CB-168-259) and Bethlem Discharge Register (DDR-08-280); all at Bethlem Museum of the Mind Archive and online at Find My Past (www.findmypast.co.uk).
(With thanks to Pam Chapman for this information about her great-grandmother.)

WARTIME ISSUES

The First World War ushered in a period of upheaval and uncertainty for Britain's county lunatic asylums. Under the Asylum War Hospitals Scheme started in 1915, the Board of Control freed up approximately 12,000 beds for injured soldiers by commandeering nine asylums. The objective was to secure 'surgical and medical treatment of the most modern and efficacious character for a large number of the soldiers wounded or stricken with physical disease during the Great War'. The asylums that were taken over were quickly renamed 'War Hospitals' to remove any stigma associated with being treated in former asylum buildings.

To make room for the soldiers, the asylum patients were moved at very short notice to other institutions, many of which were already overcrowded. It must have been a bewildering time for them. The Medical Officer of Norfolk County Asylum (later Norfolk War Hospital) commented, 'To not a few the asylum had been their home for many years, some for over fifty years, some since childhood; many even had never been in a railway train … so it will be readily believed that the whole gamut of emotion was exhibited by the patients on leaving, ranging from acute distress and misery, through gay indifference, to maniacal fury and indignation.'

One of the shocking results of these forced evacuations was the abnormally high death rate in Britain's lunatic asylums during the First World War. This was caused by a number of factors including diseases such as tuberculosis, pneumonia and influenza, which easily spread in overcrowded conditions; food shortages and rationing; reduced numbers of staff to look after the patients; and fewer therapeutic activities. According to Steven Cherry in *Mental Health Care in Modern England*, the national asylum death rate 'increased from 12 per cent in 1915 to 17.6 per cent in 1917, and it exceeded 20 per cent in 1918'.

There's no doubt that the First World War increased awareness of mental illness, particularly among returning soldiers (see Chapter 9). In 1918 in the UK, there were ninety-eight county and borough asylums, fourteen mental hospitals, two military and naval hospitals, two criminal asylums, twenty-one metropolitan licensed houses, and forty-two provincial licensed houses; these institutions housed 142,000 people of unsound mind. There were also 566 private cases in single care.

Case Study: Frederick Barr

Overcrowding and reduced food rations caused serious problems for asylum patients during the First World War. Born in 1862 in Kensal Green, Frederick Barr was a blacksmith. He and his wife Mary went on to have six children together.

Frederick became mentally ill in about April 1912, cutting his throat as a result. He was suffering with mania and was admitted to Napsbury Asylum on 11 June that year. After almost eleven months, Frederick was transferred from Napsbury to Colney Hatch Asylum on 6 May 1913. The 'Particulars of the Patient to be Transferred' contains a potted history about Frederick's mental illness.

The notes state that Frederick had hallucinations of hearing and delusions of persecution. Frederick was described as 'a most dangerous man – very powerful' who became violent 'without any previous warning'. If he saw people talking together or writing, he would believe they were plotting against him. The Colney Hatch Asylum authorities were warned that Frederick 'gets delusions about certain people (whom he will murderously attack)' and that he had recently 'made an assault on a quiet man with a chamber pot'. Despite his mania, if Frederick was kept under close supervision, he could do 'much useful ward cleaning'.

On admission to Colney Hatch, Frederick was described as 'a magnificent paranoid'. The medical officer wrote: 'He tells a story of organised persecution by a group of men … with whom his wife was in league. He had seen hidden meanings in every action of hers. Says that she used to signal to these men by turning the taps, by pulling the curtains in a peculiar manner etc. He changed his room to get away from his persecution but they followed him everywhere. Thinks that his wife used to get out of bed at night and go and have connection with other men and that she was trying to ruin his daughter. Since he has been at Napsbury has been worried by voices which accused him of unnatural acts with other animals.'

Frederick Barr, who died after a scuffle with other patients at Colney Hatch Asylum in 1918. (From Colney Hatch Asylum Case Book for Male Patients 1912–1914 (H12/CH/B/13/066) at London Metropolitan Archives, City of London)

Frederick admitted he went for a man with a pan 'because this man used to write a lot and he had the thought it was directed against him'. He thought 'that all writing is connected with him and that people write letters about him. ... Says his wife used to put poison on his pipe, that he used to get convulsions all over.'

In January 1915, Frederick's hallucinations seemed to get worse. He took off his boots and threw them into the small court 'by command of the spirits' and was put to bed after seeing bulldogs in the fireplace. By April, he was still excitable and restless and was put to bed in strong clothes after striking another patient. In November, Frederick was still having delusions about his wife's immorality, saying 'she was hypnotised and in the clutches of villains'. At the time, his weight was 10 stone 7lbs.

By early May 1916, Frederick was mentally much improved and sleeping and eating well. Frederick attributed his illness to 'anxiety over his wife's health and an attack of influenza ... causing sleeplessness'. A few weeks later, however, he was again experiencing delusions regarding his wife.

A month later, it was recorded in Frederick's notes that he was suffering from 'systematised delusional insanity', saying he was the victim of conspiracy between his wife and the staff at Napsbury Asylum who caused him to be 'persecuted by psychological methods'. Frederick frequently repeated the statement that his hands were 'clean' and that he wished to 'forget the whole business'.

By February 1917, Frederick was still deluded and very rambling in his talk but worked on the coal cart. In August that year, he was restless and very voluble in interfering with other patients. Although he was described as being in moderate health, his weight had dropped to 9 stone 8lbs. In September, there is the first mention that Frederick had been violent and aggressive in 'stealing other patients' food'. By November, he was weak and suffering with pleurisy; his weight was now 8 stone 6lbs. His weight loss was probably due to a combination of reduced food rations and the detrimental effect that pleurisy had on his overall health. From the beginning of 1918, there are repeated notes about Frederick having bruises and abrasions after altercations with other patients over food.

It all came to a head on 17 July when Frederick was knocked down in a scuffle with other patients and died as a result of his injuries. According to the inquest that followed, Frederick was pushed over, 'falling with considerable violence'. He was removed to a side room by the attendant, who subsequently noticed that he did not appear to look well and sent for the medical officer. On examination it was found that 'he was suffering from paralysis of the lower extremities, and he complained of pain in the neck. No displacement of the spinal column could be made out and no signs of fracture of the skull were apparent. He was, however, treated as a case of fracture of the spine. Paralysis gradually spread and he died on the 18th at 8.50 pm.'

Before his death, Frederick admitted that he had endeavoured to snatch the food of the other patient, and that a struggle occurred in which he fell down but he also stated that 'the attendant in removing him to the side room had done so with roughness'. The attendant strongly denied that this was so, and perhaps unsurprisingly, the other attendants who were present in the ward at the time corroborated his statement. The coroner's verdict was 'that death was due to fractured cervical vertebrae caused during a scuffle with other patients and that such death was due to misadventure'. Frederick's violent death might never have happened had it not been for the food shortages and increased instances of disease in asylums, which were part and parcel of the First World War period.

Sources: Napsbury Asylum Index to Admissions: Male Patients (H50/B/01/013/A); Colney Hatch Asylum Casebook for Male Patients 1912–1914 (H12/CH/B/13/066) and Admissions Book for Male Patients 1909–1914 (H12/CH/B/25/008); all at London Metropolitan Archives, City of London.

(With thanks to Lindsay Hall for this information about her great-grandfather and to London Metropolitan Archives for assistance given in trying to locate the owner of Frederick Barr's records.)

Case Study: Elsie Hurst
Sometimes, the onset of mental illness in a relative was so sudden and the symptoms so severe and alarming that there was no question of looking after them at home. This was what happened in the case of Elsie Hurst of Tempo, Fermanagh, now in Northern Ireland.

Born in 1896, she was the daughter of a gentleman farmer. Elsie had four older siblings and two younger ones. Her mother had died in 1913, followed two years later by her elderly father. It fell to her oldest brother William to look after his younger siblings. Grief may have played a part in Elsie's mental illness although it was not mentioned in her records.

It was towards the end of the following year when life started to unravel for Elsie. On 22 December 1916, she was admitted to the Omagh District Asylum with mania. The symptoms had begun suddenly ten days earlier. On admission, she was 'restless, excited, continually talking in an incoherent fashion, frequently referring to Marconi [and] Florence Nightingale'. Elsie's attention and orientation was much impaired and she was mischievous, kicking out at the nurses and breaking furniture.

There was no history of insanity in the family and the principal cause of the illness was put down to 'adolescence' with a contributory factor being a 'movable kidney'. Earlier that year, Elsie had had a nephropexy operation to fix a mobile kidney. Her brother stated that 'she fancied her kidney was again moving' and she had had other visceral sensations.

The facts indicating insanity on the medical certificate were 'continuous talking [and] rambling, showed marked violence at times, loss of memory, insomnia, breaking & throwing articles of furniture'. It must have been very frightening, not just for Elsie but for her family too; her two youngest sisters would have been thirteen and fifteen at the time. Elsie's acute form of mania made her a difficult patient in the asylum.

On 29 December, it was recorded in her case notes that her restlessness was 'more marked even than on admission'. She was 'continually talking' and using abusive and vulgar language. Elsie would break furniture or windows and required 'constant control by nurses'. Her insomnia was complete 'unless when given hypnotics'. Poor Elsie was confused and had 'talked herself almost hoarse'. She was too inattentive to take her meals so she was spoon-fed.

By 12 January 1917, Elsie was 'not quite so restless and gets more sleep but she is incoherent and garrulous as ever using blasphemous language.' However, she was not aggressive and was eating better. Ten days later, hypnotics were no longer required to help her sleep and 'she can also fix her attention sufficiently to employ herself at needlework'. There was no progress with regard to her language and coherency. By February, Elsie was working in the laundry and 'was amenable to instructions'.

A note on 22 April records that Elsie was 'very much improved'. She was no longer talkative and rambling; instead, she was reticent and quite coherent, and she realised her position. She was also sleeping and eating well. On 12 May 1917, Elsie was discharged 'recovered' and went home in the care of her brother.

Sadly, her state of good health was not to last. In September 1918, she was admitted to the Omagh District Asylum for a second time with 'recurrent mania'. There had been a short relapse since her discharge from the asylum but the current symptoms had begun about a month earlier. The medical certificate signed by her doctor stated she was 'singing shouting and attempting to wander at large'. Her brother stated she was 'unmanageable and constantly singing & writing'.

According to the asylum medical officer, it was a case of 'almost pure mania'. Elsie was 'lively, laughing, exalted – will talk continuously for long periods flitting from subject to subject. Exhibits fleeting grandiose ideas ... going to be a nurse, a Dr., a composer of prose, poetry, music, sermons, has written 20 works since Monday last – 2 million books in Lisbellaw Library – has read most of them.' He quoted something she said: 'I'm damned if I know if I am married – how could I know I was drugged all the time.' Elsie also claimed she was frequently horsewhipped and kicked by her brother. She was 'violent if thwarted in any way' and had written 'voluminously'.

In her case notes for 23 September, it was stated that Elsie's behaviour had been good since the day after admission. She was 'gay, exalted & talkative but controls herself'. She slept well, did sewing and had a good appetite. By November, she was 'making no progress' and was extremely 'busy', bustling about and interfering with the other patients 'but never completes anything she sets hands to'. She had been writing 'or rather scribbling' heaps of manuscript and talked rapidly but coherently.

Elsie began to suffer with conjunctivitis and on 16 December, the medical officer wrote that she had been in bed since 28 November: 'Is very troublesome. Pulls the bed clothes off her. Starts shouting & singing at intervals, gets out of bed etc. Talks to herself. Thinks she sees King Edward near her.' By now, both of

Elsie's eyes were 'practically closed' due to 'irritation by her hands'.

On 16 January 1919, she was still in bed although the eye trouble had finally cleared up. Elsie was now not so restless and excited so two days later, she was allowed up. By February, she was again 'noisy obscene & abusive' and had exalted delusions of being Secretary to the Lord Mayor of London. In mid-March she was in the Refractory Division because of her behaviour, but it was now 'variable'.

On 28 March, Elsie complained of pains in her head and a sore throat, and was unwilling to go to bed but was induced to do so. She had a temperature of 101° in the morning and 103.2° in the evening, with pains all over and a severe headache. The next day, influenza was diagnosed and two days later after heart failure set in, she 'rapidly sank and died'. She was just twenty-two years old.

Sources: Omagh District Asylum Casebooks (HOS/29/1/6/30 and HOS/29/1/6/32); Register of Patients (HOS/29/1/3/9); and Register of Deaths (HOS29/1/4/3); all at Public Record Office of Northern Ireland.

(With thanks to Lorna Latham for this information about her ancestor and to the Public Record Office of Northern Ireland for permission to quote from Elsie Hurst's records.)

Eglinton Lunatic Asylum, Cork, Ireland. Wood engraving by C.D. Laing, 1852, after W. Atkins. (Wellcome Collection. CC BY)

INTER-WAR REFORMS

The system of mental healthcare in England and Wales badly needed reforming and in 1921, Montagu Lomax wrote eloquently of the deficiencies in county asylums in *The Experiences of an Asylum Doctor*. For two years (1917–18), he had worked as an assistant medical officer at Prestwich Asylum in Lancashire. This was one of the largest asylums in the UK, with nearly 3,000 patients. Lomax described the insane as 'housed in gloomy and often dilapidated barrack-asylums, more like prisons than palaces, badly fed, poorly clad, dirty and unkempt, mostly unoccupied and certainly not amused'.

He went on to describe the plight of those who were kept 'behind the table'; these were patients who were on the special suicidal list and who had to be watched at all times by the attendants. 'Behind the table' meant that the patient's freedom of movement was completely curtailed; he was 'not allowed to walk about or mix with the other patients, but must sit behind the table and against the wall, where he can be more closely watched and restrained if necessary'. The oldest attendant at Prestwich, with some thirty years' experience, explained that 'behind the table' treatment was the routine method of dealing with unruly and refractory cases in the asylum. Lomax wrote that a dozen or more patients 'sit all day with their backs to the wall, and only leave their place to satisfy their calls of nature. In front of them is an attendant always on duty. They have no amusement, no exercise, no employment. …Yet not even for meals do they change their places or surroundings.'

The 'behind the table' crowd of lunatics in the 'refractory wards' were 'Bestialised, apathetic, mutinous, greedy, malevolent – often quarrelling fiercely with each other, at meal times snatching away each other's food, or spitting into each other's plates'. Lomax claimed that this situation would be unnecessary if the patients were 'properly graded and classified, instead of all types being herded indiscriminately together'.

Although the Board of Control strongly refuted Lomax's

allegations and he was widely condemned by the psychiatric community, his book did have an influence on the Mental Treatment Act of 1930. Under the legislation, the size of asylums was limited to under 1,000 patients, a range of therapeutic programmes were introduced, certification for all was abolished and outpatient clinics and psychiatric units in general hospitals were encouraged 'for the examination of applicants as to their fitness for reception as voluntary patients into asylums'.

One of the aims of the 1930 Act was to reduce the number of long-term inmates in asylums. People could now be seen in outpatient departments in the early stages of their mental illness; they could then receive treatment without needing to be certified and compulsorily admitted to an asylum. If further treatment was required in a mental hospital, there were now three categories of patient based on ability to provide consent: voluntary, temporary and certified.

Voluntary patients could be admitted to a mental institution, regardless of their financial status, if they were able to make an application in writing to the medical superintendent. They could leave after giving seventy-two hours' written notice, or within a twenty-eight-day period. Temporary patients were those who could not provide consent for their treatment in a mental hospital. To be admitted, a written application had to be submitted by a husband, wife or other relative, along with the medical recommendation of two medical professionals. Treatment was limited to six months in the first instance but this could be extended to a year; if treatment was still required after that time, the patient became certified.

Bethlem had opened the first psychiatric outpatients department in London before the new legislation was passed. The number of these departments increased from twenty-five in 1930 to 162 by 1935. However, in 1938, there were still thirty-one private asylums in England and Wales.

In *Sweet Bells Jangled Out of Tune*, James Gardner explores the history of Sussex Lunatic Asylum. He notes the success of an outpatient clinic in Brighton started by the asylum's medical superintendent in 1927. By 1933, 'only 24 out of 661 patients attending them were eventually certified.' However, the asylum lacked an admission hospital so 'voluntary and certified patients, once admitted, had to be treated in the same wards.'

In 1930, the term 'pauper lunatic' was abolished when the Poor Law was reformed; the mentally ill whose treatment was paid for by the state became known as 'rate-aided'. The 1930s was also the decade in which new treatments emerged for mental illness, including electroconvulsive therapy (ECT), insulin coma therapy and lobotomy.

When the National Health Service was founded in 1948, mental hospitals and many registered hospitals providing mental health services were absorbed into it.

Chapter 4

MENTAL ILLNESSES

What kind of mental conditions did our ancestors suffer from to need care in an institution? In the report of the Metropolitan Commissioners in Lunacy of 1844, the 'principal forms of insanity' usually found in lunatic asylums were identified. They were mania, dementia, melancholia, monomania, moral insanity, congenital idiocy and congenital imbecility, general paralysis of the insane and epilepsy.

First on the list was mania, which was subdivided into acute mania or raving madness; ordinary mania or chronic madness of a less acute form; and periodical or remittent mania with comparatively lucid intervals. Acute mania was the first stage of the disease, in which there was a great deal of excitement, restlessness, a confusion of ideas and 'vehemence of feeling and expression'.

After a period of acute mania, the symptoms of many sufferers became milder, leading to chronic mania. The Commissioners found that a large proportion of patients in lunatic asylums were chronic maniacs with delusions and hallucinations; they were mostly harmless and could be employed in work therapy and undertake amusements. The Commissioners were keen to stress that 'however quiet and manageable they may appear to be under the authority and supervision to which they are subjected in an Asylum, they are quite unfit to be at large and to mix with ordinary society.' Mania was one of the most difficult mental illnesses to manage because sufferers could be a danger to themselves or others when they were going through a period of great excitement or violence.

Dementia came next in the report and was defined as the 'decay and obliteration of the intellectual faculties'; mania was frequently a prelude to it. In dementia, all the powers of the mind were lost. Patients might have memory disorders, personality changes and impaired reasoning as a result of brain disease or injury. It was sometimes the 'primary form of derangement' and could be caused by overwhelming grief, old age, destitution and poverty. Dementia could also develop after apoplexy, epilepsy, paralysis 'and other affections of the brain'. The Commissioners described mania and dementia as 'the prevailing forms of insanity' in most large asylums. The report cited Lancaster County Asylum where 418 patients, or about two-thirds of the whole number, were suffering with mania or dementia.

Third on the list was melancholia, another condition in which there were varying degrees of symptoms. Many melancholics had a lowness of spirits 'with a distaste for the pleasures of life, and a total indifference to its concerns'. They had no delusions, hallucinations or any disorder of their intellectual powers, but they frequently experienced highs and lows in their feelings. For these melancholics, there was a good chance of recovery from mental illness.

The despondency in other patients with melancholia was caused by their belief that they had suffered 'some unreal misfortune'. According to the Lunacy Commissioners, 'Many are convinced that they have committed unpardonable sins … [whilst] others believe themselves to be accused or suspected of some heinous crime. … Some fancy that they have sustained great pecuniary losses, and are utterly and irretrievably ruined.' In addition, a great number of those with melancholy believed they were suffering with 'some terrible bodily disease' when, in fact, they had 'some complaint of which they magnify the symptoms'.

Large numbers of melancholics were committed to lunatic asylums because they were at a high risk of suicide 'from a disgust of life'; they required constant supervision and a great deal of care.

Unlike mania, patients with monomania retained their power of reasoning, except about one particular idea, interest or topic over which they obsessed. Sometimes called partial mania, the condition was further sub-divided into categories, for example, monomania of pride, in which the sufferer had delusions of grandeur. There was also monomania of suspicion, of fear and of superstition; a common delusion of monomaniacs was that they could talk to supernatural beings.

Man suffering from melancholia at West Riding Lunatic Asylum, circa 1869. (Wellcome Collection. CC BY)

Fifth on the Commissioners' list was moral insanity, a form of mental disease 'in which the affections, sentiments, habits and, generally speaking, the moral feelings of the mind, rather than the intellectual faculties, are in an unsound and disordered state'. Patients with moral insanity experienced a 'total want of self-control, with an inordinate propensity to excesses of various kinds, among others, habitual intoxication'. According to the 1844 report, there were many female asylum patients 'whose disorder principally consists in a moral perversion connected with hysterical or sexual excitement'.

Case Study: Annie Gallagher

When mental illness struck young people, it could be the cruellest of diseases; it deprived them of their futures and often meant the rest of their lives were spent in asylums.

Annie Gallagher was just nineteen when she became ill in 1914. The youngest of eight children, she lived in Wigan with her parents and siblings, and worked as a stocking knitter. In March of that year, she became very quiet and gradually got worse; this was in contrast to her usual personality. There was no previous history of mental illness in the family and Annie had been intelligent in school, reaching Standard VI.

Early in July 1914, Annie started exhibiting other symptoms and at some point, she was admitted to the Infirmary in Wigan. An attendant there reported that 'Annie Gallagher fancies she has lost her voice. Screams in the early morning, laughing, crying & muttering to herself at times. Refuses food. Attempts to run away.'

Annie was admitted to the County Lunatic Asylum at Rainhill, Merseyside on 13 August 1914. No causes were identified on her admission notes. Under 'mental state on admission', she was described as a 'nervous and fidgety girl, who sits up in bed glancing about the room and constantly fiddling with the bedclothes. She is with difficulty persuaded to whisper an occasional answer to questions, but little information can be obtained from her. She has no idea of time or place. She is constantly chattering to herself and after repeated questioning says she is talking to a relation. She has shown no suicidal or other impulses since admission. She does not associate with the other patients and is uninterested in her surroundings. She sleeps well, takes her food well and is clean in her habits.'

In August 1914, her case notes list 'mania' as her diagnosis. She was conversing 'with imaginary persons. She whispers when questioned. She is very confused. She says "they put stuff in her food".' On 29 August, Annie was 'aurally hallucinated and takes no interest in anything'. By November 1914, she was still confused but was 'working satisfactorily in the laundry'. A month later, she was 'too dull and confused' to do any work.

By July 1915, Annie had become wet and dirty in her habits and at times, she was 'excitable and impulsive'. Her memory was failing too, saying that she had been in the asylum for two years when she had been a patient for less than twelve months.

A year later, the medical officer wrote that Annie was now 'almost devoid of intellect' and 'impulsive & liable to strike out without any provocation'. Although she was clean, she did no work. In January 1918, there was no apparent change in Annie, mental or physical, and by 1921, the diagnosis was changed to

'Primary Dementia'. Annie enjoyed fairly good physical health as her various ailments were treated over the years, but sadly her mind never returned. She remained at Rainhill until her death of dementia praecox (premature dementia) on 19 August 1942, twenty-eight years after she was first admitted.

Sources: Rainhill County Lunatic Asylum Admission Papers (M614 RAI/1/50); Annexe Casebooks: Female Patients (M614 RAI/9/10); Death and Discharge Book: Female Patients (M614 RAI/10/28); all at Liverpool Record Office.

(With thanks to Mike Gallagher for this information about his great-aunt, and to Liverpool Record Office for permission to quote from Annie Gallagher's records.)

IDIOTS AND IMBECILES

Congenital idiocy and congenital imbecility were also regularly seen in lunatic asylums. Congenital idiots were those whose intellectual faculties had never been developed. Colloquial terms for idiots also included 'fools' and 'naturals'. By contrast, congenital imbeciles had experienced some kind of defect after birth that made them feeble-minded. They could exercise their minds in a limited way and today, such patients would be described as being learning disabled.

People suffering from congenital conditions who could not be cared for by their relatives might be sent to a workhouse or asylum instead. There were many different degrees of imbecility but generally, it was the most extreme cases that were admitted to lunatic asylums whilst harmless imbeciles were accommodated in workhouses. In the mid- to late nineteenth century, there was increasing concern about the housing of idiots in county lunatic asylums. In 1884, the medical superintendent at Prestwich Lunatic Asylum pointed out that 'The habits and ways of adult lunatics make it most desirable that children of such tender years should not be forced into close companionship with them ...'

The authorities at the Somerset County Lunatic Asylum argued that 'Idiots are teachable and imitative, and either acquire bad habits

Claybury Asylum, Woodford Bridge, Middlesex, opened in 1893. (Author's collection)

and lessen their small intelligence if they are neglected, or, on the other hand, if properly cared for, improve, and will, many of them, be able to maintain themselves.'

Gradually, asylums exclusively for idiots and imbeciles were founded, including the Earlswood Asylum at Redhill, Surrey in 1847 and the Royal Albert Asylum at Lancaster in 1868 (see Chapter 8). However, there were never sufficient places in these specialist asylums and idiots and imbeciles continued to be housed in workhouses and lunatic asylums.

Case Study: James Pattenden

Venereal disease, including syphilis, was a common problem in members of the British Army and Royal Navy. James Pattenden joined the army as a private in 1879 at the age of eighteen. He had previously been a butcher in Hounslow and in his army medical history was described as 'temperate' with 'very good' habits. In January 1881, he was posted to India. A year later, he was hospitalised in Jubbulpore (Jabalpur) in the Central Provinces with 'Syph. Prim.'. This was primary syphilis, the first stage of the disease, during which James would have had genital sores, later called chancres. The contagion was described as mild but he spent twenty-two days in hospital being treated with a potassium iodide tincture.

There is no further mention of syphilis in his army medical record, yet he received hospital treatment for other complaints such as ague and gonorrhoea. Although potassium iodide was the standard treatment for syphilis at the time, it was ineffective. The early symptoms would have disappeared by themselves within a few weeks, leading the sufferer to believe he or she had been cured. Instead, the bacterium stayed in the body, only to reappear months or years later. This happened in James's case because more than twenty years later, he was diagnosed with general paralysis of the insane (GPI).

In 1885, James was posted back to Britain and was in the Army Reserve Leicester Regiment. He married Harriet Passey in Croydon in 1887, and by 1891, he had left the army and was a police constable. The couple went on to have eight children, one of whom died in infancy.

By about 1898, James started to suffer with memory loss. In May 1900, he was admitted to Fisherton House Asylum in Salisbury; he would have been sent there by Croydon Union after first being admitted to the infirmary. It would have been nigh on impossible for Harriet to visit her husband so far from home. At that time, Croydon did not have its own asylum, sending its paupers to Fisherton, Cane Hill Asylum and the Isle of Wight instead. According to the Lunacy Patients' Admission Registers, James was discharged from Fisherton in November of the same year 'recovered'.

At the time of the 1901 census, James was still at home but described as a retired police constable 'unemployed', which is perhaps unsurprising given his symptoms of memory loss and difficulty with speech. His wife Harriet was trying to make ends meet by working as a cook. This must have been a very difficult time for her, trying to provide for the family, look after her husband and tend to her seven children, four of whom were under the age of six.

At some point, James was re-admitted to the Croydon Union Infirmary and in July 1903, he was sent to the new Croydon Mental Hospital, which had opened a month earlier. The medical certificate stated that James was 'Very depressed at times. Has delusions of having great wealth, promises extravagant presents to everyone & wants to telegraph to everybody. Says God has sent down angels in answer to his prayers to forgive everyone's sins. Says he can see them all round him. That God has given him power to heal all diseases.'

George Stenton, the head attendant at Croydon Union Infirmary, added that James was alternately depressed and excited. He 'walks round the Ward attempting to heal all the patients. Promises them a house & numerous other things.' Another delusion James had was that his two daughters were living at the asylum and that he could see and hear them talking; in fact, he had four daughters, not two.

James was described as cheerful but irritable, temperate and steady. The case notes reveal his gradual decline into dementia and loss of faculties, which was a classic feature of tertiary stage syphilis. A few months after admission, he was 'more lost in his intellect now and cannot appreciate any questions put to him. He is very weak and uncertain in his gait and actions.'

By March 1904, James was 'absolutely demented, wet and dirty' but was 'well nourished & takes his food'. Just over a year later, in April 1905, in a Report to the Commissioners in Lunacy, the medical officer wrote, 'He is the subject of General Paralysis. Demented, Wet & Dirty. Has to have everything done for him. Deluded. Thinks that he is Lord Mayor of Croydon. He is in Bad Health & condition. Emaciated.'

By now, James was in the advanced stage of general paralysis with his bodily condition affected as well as his mind. He died on 1 October 1905 of general paralysis and lobar pneumonia, aged forty-two. Sadly, James's wife had died earlier that year in March, and their children, aged between six and seventeen, were split up.

Sources: Croydon Mental Hospital Casebooks (CWA-01/174, CWA-01/175 and CWA-01/176); all at Bethlem Museum of the Mind Archive and online at Find My Past (www.findmypast.co.uk).
(With thanks to Val Preece for this information about her great-uncle.)

GENERAL PARALYSIS OF THE INSANE

General paralysis or paresis of the insane, or GPI, was another 'principle form of insanity' described in the 1844 report. At the time, no one knew for sure what caused it. The Commissioners noted that the disease rarely occurred in women and was the result of 'a debauched and intemperate life'. The condition was distinct from ordinary paralysis and its duration was 'scarcely ever longer than two or at most three years, when it generally brings its victim to the grave'.

The Commissioners described the symptoms:

The onset of the disease is distinguished by an impediment in the articulation, an effort is required in speaking, and the words are uttered with a sort of mumbling, and stammering. At this period, there is no other perceptible sign of paralysis, and the mobility of the limbs is not at all impaired. In a second stage, the patient is observed to have a tottering gait: the limbs are weaker than in health, especially the lower extremities, while the functions of the organs of sense are likewise enfeebled. In the progress of time, a third stage appears, during which the victim of this malady loses not only the power of locomotion but can neither feed himself nor answer the calls of nature. He becomes more and more weak and emaciated.

The disorder of the mind was generally a type of monomania, in which the individual affected fancies himself possessed of vast riches and power. The prognosis for GPI patients was hopeless; it was always fatal within two or three years of diagnosis, but it was usually a secondary disease such as gangrene, pneumonia, heart failure or apoplexy that caused the deaths of sufferers.

According to the physician at Edinburgh Asylum writing in 1876, the only good thing about the disease was that 'the patient is almost never conscious of his condition or his prospects, but is usually preternaturally happy and exalted, and that its duration seldom exceeds two or three years.'

Although a link with general paralysis of the insane and syphilis was suspected from the 1850s, it was not until the Edwardian period that it could be proved. In 1905, *Spirochaeta pallida*, the bacterium that caused syphilis, was identified and found in the brain of a patient who had died of GPI. The following year, the Wassermann test was introduced leading to many positive results from GPI patients; unfortunately, the test also produced plenty of inaccurate results too.

By this time, it was generally accepted that general paralysis of the insane was caused by tertiary syphilis. Despite this, there was no effective treatment for syphilis until 1909, when Salvarsan, a compound of toxic arsenic, was developed. Until then, mercurial compounds such as iodide of potassium and mercury were used to treat the symptoms of the disease, and malaria fever therapy was also used during the 1920s to treat GPI. It was not until the advent of penicillin in the 1940s that syphilis was finally brought under control.

EPILEPTICS

Epilepsy was another condition highlighted in the Lunacy Commissioners' Report of 1844 because many mentally ill patients in asylums were also epileptics. The report acknowledged there were some epileptics in asylums 'who are not insane, or in any way disordered in mind during the intervals of their paroxysms'. This rarely happened with adults but there were known instances with children 'when they have become a source of anxiety and trouble to their parents, as well as dangerous to themselves [and] have sometimes been sent by Boards of Guardians to Asylums for protection'. The Commissioners did not consider this a sufficient reason for associating sane epileptics with the insane. Instead, they preferred a proper classification scheme where there were epileptic wards separate from the insane but they noted that 'there are many Lunatic Asylums where this regulation is entirely neglected.'

Apart from sane epileptics, there were generally three types of epileptic patients in asylums: epileptic idiots, epileptic imbeciles and epileptic maniacs. Epileptic idiots required great care because they were so prone to having accidents. According to the Lunacy Commissioners, epileptic imbecility was usually a result of very frequent and severe fits over a long period of time, which impaired the intellectual faculties.

Some patients with epileptic mania were prone to violence when a fit was coming on, becoming 'irritable, morose, malicious and sometimes exceedingly dangerous'. A small number of epileptics were subject to acute mania, usually a day or two after a fit or sometimes immediately afterwards. The patient would be 'seized with a sudden fury, during which he sings, roars, shrieks, or resembles a man in a violent fit of intoxication'. The type of madness that was complicated with epilepsy was said to be 'one of the most mischievous and dangerous forms of the disease'.

Sane epileptics accommodated in workhouses were more likely to be surrounded by other sane inmates, but they usually received better care when looked after in an asylum because there was more staff.

FORM 21.

WILTS COUNTY ASYLUM.

NOTICE OF DEATH.

Date of Reception Order, the *16th* day of *Jan 1891*

I hereby give you Notice, that *Jane Brixey*

a —————— Patient received into this Asylum on the *17th*

day of *January* 1891, died therein on the *19th*

day of *February* 1913

(Signed) *James Turner*

Clerk of Asylum.

Dated the *Nineteenth* day of *February* 1913

To ——Case Book.——————————

Statement Respecting the Above-Named Patient.

Name ——*Jane Brixey*

Sex and Age ——*Female, 61 years*

Married, Single or Widowed ——*Married*

Profession or Occupation ——*Wife of a Labourer*

Place of abode immediately before being placed under care and treatment (if known). } *Bemerton*

Apparent Cause of Death } *Primary. Fatty Degeneration of Heart. Secondary Cerebral Tumour*

Whether or not ascertained by post mortem examination. } *Yes*

Time and any unusual circumstances attending the death; also a description of any injuries known to exist at time of death, or found subsequently on body of deceased. } *8.14 am* *None* *None*

Duration of disease of which patient died *2 Years (2 Yrs..*

Names and description of persons present at the death. } *Louisa M. Freece (Nurse)*

Whether or not mechanical restraint was applied to deceased within seven days previous to death, with its character and duration if so applied. } *No*

I hereby certify that the particulars contained in the above statement are true.

(Signed) *J. Ireland Bowes.*

Medical Officer of Asylum.

Death notice for Jane Brixey, who died in 1913 at Wiltshire County Lunatic Asylum. (With thanks to Alan Weeks and Wiltshire & Swindon Archives)

Case Study: Jane Brixey

Severe epileptic fits could bring about significant memory loss and for Jane Brixey née Hardiman, they led to an irreversible decline in her mental health. The daughter of a Wiltshire carter born in 1852, she had gone into domestic service and later married George Brixey, a labourer, at Burcombe on 27 March 1875. At the time of her marriage, Jane was working as a servant for a veterinary surgeon in a neighbouring parish.

All seemed to be going well. By the 1881 census, the couple were living at Sidney Cottages, Bemerton. They had no children but George was now a brickmaker whilst Jane was working as a domestic. At some point in 1887, she started having epileptic fits, which gradually became more frequent and serious. Two years later, she had to give up domestic work for Mrs Farrant at Belvedere House, not far from where Jane lived.

By January 1891, a crisis was reached and Jane was admitted to Wiltshire County Lunatic Asylum in Devizes at the age of thirty-nine with 'Epileptic Imbecility'. According to her admission record, Jane had 'enjoyed good health, has no infectious diseases, been fairly well off, had no domestic trouble or mental anxiety, and led a moral and temperate life'. She had also had a fairly good education.

Yet her frequent epileptic fits had made her mind and memory weak, and on admission to the asylum, she had a vacant expression with a 'confused & childish manner'; she also had difficulty in understanding questions and in expressing herself. A neighbour said she had 'found her in a fit with a kettle of boiling water pouring over her & that she has frequently found her lying on the fender'. According to Jane, she usually remained semi-conscious for some time after a fit. She said that she intended to stop working for Mrs Farrant, although she had not done any work for her for eighteen months.

In Jane's admission register entry, the medical officer noted she had 'a general papular eruption probably from bromide treatment she received before admission'. This indicates that another doctor, probably a Poor Law medical officer, had attempted to treat her fits with potassium bromide; this was regularly used at the time as a sedative and anticonvulsant to control seizures.

Sadly for Jane, the prognosis on her mental condition was deemed 'almost hopeless'. In the days after admission, she didn't know where she was; she wandered in conversation and had hallucinations of sight and hearing at night. Her fits were frequent and severe so she was prescribed potassium bromide (K Br).

By April, Jane was 'noisy & excited, making amorous overtures to the A.M.O. [Assistant Medical Officer]'. She 'wanders about her room all day packing her bedding into a bundle & saying she must prepare to go home.' In October, the Medical Officer experimented with her medication, discontinuing the potassium bromide. By January 1892, he made the note: 'Without treatment 50 days, 51 fits; with K Br 50 days, 1 fit.'

By strange coincidence, Jane's husband George was also admitted to the Wiltshire County Lunatic Asylum. He became a patient in January 1892 when he developed epileptic mania, but he died there in October the same year.

Gradually, Jane's fits lessened but sadly her memory and mind did not return. By December 1894, her diagnosis was changed to 'Epileptic Mania'. Jane was now 'very suspicious of all around her, always irritable and quarrelsome. Childish manner and her mind and memory are much impaired.' She had also developed chronic bronchitis. In November 1897, it was reported that she 'has not taken K Br for a long time past & fits seem to have ceased'. The last fit was induced five years earlier 'by fright of Guy Fawkes'. There had been no apparent cause for the seizures to start; there was no heredity and Jane had not had convulsions as a child.

Jane's mental condition remained unchanged and she had

various ailments, which were dealt with by the asylum staff. However, by 1905, she was 'depressed & hypochondriacal' and was jealous of the attention paid to other patients. In 1910, her diagnosis was changed to 'Epileptic Dementia'. Jane continued to make herself useful in the ward when she was able and took 'a good deal of kindly interest in a little imbecile who works in the sewing room with her'.

In February 1913, twenty-two years after she was first admitted to the asylum, Jane died aged sixty-one. A post-mortem revealed the cause of death was fatty degeneration of the heart and a cerebral tumour.

Sources: Wiltshire County Lunatic Asylum Patient Admission Register (J4/170/6); Female Patients' Casebook (J4/191/14/3); and Register of Deaths (J4/177/1); all at Wiltshire and Swindon Archives.

(With thanks to Alan Weeks for this information about his great-great-aunt and to Wiltshire and Swindon Archives for permission to quote from Jane Brixey's records.)

CAUSES OF MENTAL ILLNESS

All lunatic asylums had to produce annual reports including statistics compiled by the medical superintendent listing the forms of insanity admitted during the year, and their attributed causes. As an example, in 1881, in seventy-nine of the cases at Aberdeen, no cause could be attributed. Fifty-two of the cases were caused by 'Hereditary Predisposition' whilst seventeen (most of whom were male patients) were a result of intemperance. The remaining forty-nine cases were attributed to a wide variety of causes including childbirth (puerperal mania), death of friends, epilepsy, disappointment in love, over-anxiety, lactation and 'climacteric change [the menopause]'.

There was an inextricable link between poverty and attacks of mental illness in working-class patients. In 1875, at the Somerset County Pauper Lunatic Asylum, patients admitted with 'stress of poverty' as the cause of their insanity only received dietetical treatment in the infirmary wards. In their annual report, the administrators found that 'better living and more cheerful surroundings' were all these patients needed. They argued that this proved more needed to be done by parochial officers 'to meet the requirements primarily affecting the bodily health of patients prior to admission'.

In many cases, the causes of mental illness were attributed to a 'hereditary disposition' if, on investigation, a member of the patient's family had been mentally ill. Other mental illnesses were attributed to exposure to toxic metals, which were a hazard of a large number of Victorian occupations. This could include mercury poisoning in hatters, furriers and mirror-makers; lead poisoning in white lead and pottery workers; and copper poisoning in the tin industry.

Case Study: Ann Rebecca Mais
Heredity was one cause of mental illness that asylum medical officers always checked for on admission. However, they could only go by the information provided by relatives, who did not always know the full details.

It's quite likely that Ann Rebecca Mais' insanity was hereditary. Born in Kingston, Jamaica in 1787, she was one of five children from a relationship between Charles Mais, a merchant and plantation owner, and Anne Ivey, a quadroon and free mulatto woman. In the early 1790s, Charles returned to his native Bristol with his children, leaving Anne behind. Back in Britain, Charles married three times, having nine children altogether. Five of them, including Ann Rebecca, would go on to suffer with mental illness and end their lives in lunatic asylums, although two probably experienced dementia-type symptoms in old age.

It's not clear when Ann Rebecca's problems first started but she was admitted to Droitwich Asylum in November 1810 at the age of twenty-three. Droitwich was a private madhouse run by William Ricketts that had been founded twenty years earlier. At the time, Ann Rebecca was living in Bristol and there were other private asylums closer to home, such as Fishponds, opened in 1760. Perhaps William Ricketts' establishment had been personally recommended to someone in Ann Rebecca's family. Unfortunately, few records for the Droitwich Asylum have survived before 1836 so very little detail is known about her admission.

Further clues can be found in a register for the Worcester County Asylum at Powick, to which Ann Rebecca was admitted in September 1871. By now, she was eighty-four and her diagnosis was 'monomania of suspicion'. The notes record this was her first attack of mental illness, of sixty-one years' duration due to an unknown cause. She wasn't epileptic, suicidal or dangerous to others. The Worcester register notes: 'Her certificate says she fancies she is being murdered and robbed, states everyone is against her, believes everyone touching her defiles her and would wash all her eatables to remove contamination from the Cook's touch if allowed.'

She had been an inmate of Droitwich Asylum since 1810, and was of a good family but 'has no means'. This last comment could explain why Ann Rebecca was transferred from Droitwich to Worcester. When she was first admitted to Droitwich, she certainly did have money of her own as she had been left gifts in the will of her grandfather, who died in 1803. On the various censuses, she was described as a 'gentlewoman' and an 'owner of property'. It's likely that after sixty-one years of treatment, her money had simply run out and she was now admitted as a pauper chargeable to the Droitwich Poor Law Union.

The notes for Ann Rebecca's time at Worcester reveal how her mental illness made her a difficult patient. Although she was in good bodily health considering her age, 'a physical examination of her various systems is impracticable as she forcibly resists being touched especially by the doctors.' She seldom ate beef and objected to 'animal food' so her diet consisted chiefly of milk, gravy, eggs, vegetables and farinaceous (starchy) food.

Occasionally, it was difficult to give her sufficient nourishment 'owing to her aversion to many articles of diet'.

By July 1872, Ann Rebecca was free from a troublesome cough and in better physical health. The medical superintendent wrote that she 'has few ideas respecting anything and resists any attempt on the part of the medical attendant to examine her condition'. She used 'strong language if one persists in pressing attentions on her, wishes to say "good morning" so as to get rid of me, will offer violence if an attempt be made to feel her pulse'.

In January 1873, bronchitis and emphysema were causing Ann Rebecca considerable trouble and making her very feeble, although she was still able to be up daily. By September, she was 'often very cross & ill-natured' and 'in a debilitated & delicate state' but able to get up for a few hours a day. In January 1875, the medical superintendent wrote that Ann Rebecca 'had been confined to bed for some time owing to her debilitated & feeble state & on account of cough & shortness of breath'. She was being given a stimulant nutritious diet and a stimulating expectorant mixture.

Finally, on 9 March 1875, Ann Rebecca died from chronic bronchitis, emphysema of many years' duration, and debility and degeneration of old age. She was almost eighty-eight years old and had spent nearly sixty-five years in lunatic asylums.

Sources: Droitwich Asylum Admission Register (Ref: 125 BA 710); Worcester County Lunatic Asylum Pauper Admissions (Ref: 489:16 BA 8343); Worcester County Lunatic Asylum Patients' Case Papers (Ref: 599.4 BA13237); Worcester County Lunatic Asylum Register of Deaths (Ref: 489:16 BA 8343); all at Worcestershire Archive and Archaeology Service.

(With thanks to Howard Mais for this information about his ancestor, and to Worcestershire Health and Care NHS Trust and Worcestershire Archive and Archaeology Service for permission to quote from Ann Rebecca Mais' records.)

CLASSIFICATION OF PATIENTS

In the asylums of the eighteenth century, inmates had been accommodated in rows of single cells that led off from long galleries; these, in turn, doubled up as day rooms for those who had more liberty but it meant that patients congregated together regardless of their condition or behaviour. By contrast, the architecture of Victorian asylums reflected the need to implement a complex classification scheme if patients were to be treated effectively. The new designs incorporated dormitories for the quiet and convalescent, single rooms for refractory and 'watched' cases, and separate recreation rooms. The classification system aided the recovery of patients and at the same time, made it easier for the asylum staff to manage them.

'Senile dementia' patient at West Riding Lunatic Asylum. (Wellcome Collection. CC BY)

In their 1844 report, the Lunacy Commissioners described the classification of patients in well-regulated asylums: 'It consists in the distribution of patients with reference to their mental disorders, and in associating those persons whose intercourse is likely to be mutually beneficial, and in separating others who are in a state that renders their society a source of mutual irritation and annoyance.' This meant separating dangerous lunatics from the others, the 'restless, noisy and agitated' from the quiet, and the dirty (those who were incontinent) from the clean. Melancholic patients, especially those who were suicidal, were said to be most at risk if they were associated with demented or violent maniacs. The epileptic patients and those who were tranquil and convalescent needed to be kept apart from the noisy and excited. Males were always separated from females, and the incurable from the curable.

The Lunacy Commissioners highlighted the complex and successful classification scheme at Lancaster, where there were ten wards on each side of the asylum. Here, the patients with dementia were associated with and assisted by the 'active, orderly and quiet cases'. Those who were suicidal were associated with the 'cheerful and watchful' cases.

However, the scheme at Gloucester County Asylum was said to be the most representative of other institutions around the country, except for the fact it separated epileptics, which most asylums did not do. At Gloucester, there were five classes of patient: quiet patients and those who were almost convalescent; the epileptics; the fatuous (idiots and imbeciles); the dirty and noisy; and the convalescents and some incurables who were 'capable of employment, and are occupied in cultivating the garden and grounds'.

At the Aberdeen Royal Lunatic Asylum, there were many separate and detached buildings, which enabled the staff to enforce the classification of patients into different groups. The annual report for 1888 commented that patients were 'distributed in sitting rooms and parlours of moderate size, having constant access at pleasure to the open air, and not in large halls and galleries with only periodic egress'. As the patients had a liberal diet and warm clothing, they were able to 'combat the insidious effects of the east winds while still enjoying the benefit of fresh air'. The 'most disagreeable cases' were isolated at night in single bedrooms to avoid disrupting the other patients.

According to Roy Porter in *The Cambridge Illustrated History of Medicine*, asylum keepers had to establish 'pathways of progress' so that 'improving lunatics could move, stage by stage, nearer the exit' whilst chronic cases occupied the wards at the back. It was a real challenge to achieve this while maintaining economy and discipline.

Porter describes the new 'science of asylum management' practised by the medical superintendents and assistant medical officers. Psychiatry was still in its infancy but the Association of Medical Officers of Asylums and Hospitals for the Insane was founded in 1841. The organisation had its own publication, entitled *Journal of Mental Science*, which helped to develop the profession. The Association changed its name to the Medico-Psychological Association in 1865 and to the Medico-Psychological Association of Great Britain and Ireland in 1887; the organisation became the Royal College of Psychiatrists in 1971.

Chapter 5

INSIDE THE ASYLUM

After 1774, a person had to be medically certified before being admitted to an asylum, although this did not apply to paupers. From 1832, an order for admission by a magistrate was needed for pauper patients; this became known as a 'reception order'. After 1890, for both pauper and private patients, the signatures of two doctors were required on a medical certificate, as well as a reception order from a magistrate. Voluntary patients could be admitted without a reception order because they were not certified as being insane.

If your ancestor was admitted to a lunatic asylum, he or she would have experienced a similar admission procedure that was common to all mental institutions. Asylum patients were bathed and weighed on arrival, and a detailed record was made of their medical and physical condition. They were then dressed in asylum clothing and their own clothes were stored until such time as they were discharged. If anyone was found to have an infectious disease, they would be kept in quarantine in the infirmary; in such cases, the patient's own clothing would have to be destroyed.

Each asylum was slightly different in terms of layout. The design would usually have followed the 'Suggestions and Instructions' issued by the Lunacy Commission for local authorities, offering advice on asylum architecture and the layout of grounds. The Commissioners preferred a 'modified traditional country house estate' in a rural setting, with an acre for every four patients. They advised that 'the buildings should be surrounded with land sufficient to afford out-door employment for the male, and exercise for all the patients, and to protect them from being overlooked, or disturbed by strangers.' It was specified that airing courts be built next to the asylum and within the boundary walls for daily exercise.

The treatment for mental illness in the Victorian period relied largely on keeping the mind and body occupied through work therapy, exercise and entertainment. A nutritious diet was also prescribed, as were drugs, when necessary, to calm patients.

WORK THERAPY

In a county asylum, a great part of the patients' day would be spent working, if they were well enough to do so. As they were usually built in the countryside, most Victorian asylums could become self-sufficient estates, running their own farms, laundries and workshops. Work therapy in horticulture and agriculture was widely used in asylums.

The medical superintendent at the Prestwich Asylum argued that 'Success in the treatment of the insane, apart from the medical treatment, largely depends upon the perfection of the appliances in an Asylum for fully engaging all patients who are physically capable of employment, in one sort of occupation.' As well as restoring 'hundreds of curable patients to perfect health', work therapy prevented others from sinking into a lower state of mental illness.

At the Surrey County Lunatic Asylum, male patients worked in the garden, the farm, the kitchen, the wards, the laundry, in the engine house and in sawing and chopping firewood. Others did specialist work as shoemaking, tailoring, carpentry, bricklaying, painting, baking, mat-making and straw-working.

Female patients were equally industrious, working in the laundry and kitchen, doing sewing and knitting, working in the wards, and creating straw and fancy work. According to the annual report in 1848, they repaired and made numerous articles for the asylum including 930 handkerchiefs, 259 caps, 256 shifts and 173 aprons. In addition, they created work for the bazaar such as bunches of artificial flowers, cravats, shirts and nightgowns; these items were

'Gardening at St Luke's' in 'Lunatic London'. (From Living London, *1902)*

sold and the money was given to the patients leaving the asylum on recovery.

As asylums became more and more overcrowded, it became increasingly difficult to provide work for all those who were able, especially for the male patients. Wherever possible, extra land was purchased by asylums on which patients could labour.

In 1888, when extra accommodation was needed for the inmates of the overcrowded Aberdeen Royal Asylum, the managers bought a large estate consisting of new and old mansion houses and 283 acres. This became a branch of the institution at Daviot for male and female pauper patients who were accustomed to agricultural and other outdoor labour. At Daviot, it was thought that the 'conditions under which the inmates live and work are ideal'. The estate was self-supporting and was able to provide butcher meat, vegetables and flowers for the main Royal Asylum.

At Bethlem and St Luke's, the patients were from the educated or professional classes so it was not considered socially acceptable to find them bodily work to do, unlike in the county asylums (although at St Luke's, some of the inmates did gardening). Instead, patients at Bethlem were encouraged in the cultivation of music, painting and literary composition to occupy their minds and restore their confidence; there was even a quarterly magazine entitled *Under the Dome*. In the recreation room, all manner of entertainments were put on in the evenings, from plays, dances, 'socials' and concerts staged by the orchestra made up of doctors, attendants and inmates.

THE DAILY DIET

Contrary to earlier thinking when patients were half-starved to keep them weak, a liberal, nutritious diet was now considered an essential part of treatment for the mentally ill, many of whom were in a poor, physical condition on arrival.

In 1849, at the Surrey County Lunatic Asylum, breakfast consisted of 1 pint of milk porridge and 6oz of bread for males and 4oz for females. Supper was exactly the same. Dinner was the only meal that varied. On Mondays, it was soup thickened with barley, peas and vegetables, plus 6oz of bread. On Tuesdays, Saturdays and Sundays, dinner consisted of 6oz of boiled or roast beef or mutton, free from bone, with 4oz of bread, vegetables and ¾ of a pint of beer.

On Wednesdays, baked or boiled suet pudding was served with 16oz for males and 12oz for females, plus ¾ of a pint of beer. Thursday was meat pie day with vegetables and ¾ of a pint of beer, whilst Friday's dinner was baked rice pudding with treacle.

Working patients were entitled to extras in their daily diet. The men received a luncheon of bread and cheese, plus ¾ of a pint of beer each, while the female patients had ½ a pint of beer each. All of the women in employment were given 2oz of tea, 8oz of sugar and 6oz of butter every week.

Similar dietaries were in operation at lunatic asylums around the UK. In 1870 at the Berkshire County Lunatic Asylum, breakfast and supper was bread, butter and tea. The soup, which was offered once a week, was made from 'Legs of Beef, Fresh Beef Bones, New Zealand Mutton, Peas, Carrots, Turnips, Onions & c.'

The kitchen at Claybury Asylum, Woodford, Essex. Photograph by the London & County Photographic Co., circa 1893. (Wellcome Collection. CC BY)

EXERCISE AND RECREATION

Exercise was considered essential to an asylum patient's daily routine. Airing courts with high walls were part of the design of the first lunatic asylums; later, it became more important to have larger open spaces for recreation. At Lancaster, the wards opened out onto airing grounds, which were accessible to the patients for at least three hours in the morning and three hours in the afternoon when the weather was favourable. Most of the patients who were able, 'go regularly beyond the airing-courts for exercise'; some went beyond the asylum grounds and a select few walked 'on parole' where they pleased unattended.

Keeping the patients entertained and engaged with recreational activities was an important part of asylum treatment in the second half of the nineteenth century. At the Aberdeen Asylum during 1881, 'twenty cricket matches were played against various clubs of the town.' There were also frequent assemblies for dancing and performances were given by the Aberdeen Amateur Opera Company and the Kean Dramatic Society.

At the Somerset County Pauper Lunatic Asylum, the patients participated in cricket in the summer and football in the winter, as well as 'numerous dramatic representations'. Along with a variety of daily papers and periodicals, there were a number of games available for evening amusement such as draughts, dominoes and cards. Asylums seem to have been one of the few Victorian institutions to allow cards; they were banned in workhouses, prisons and hospitals because they were associated with gambling.

Regular dances and balls, as well as concerts, were staged, often by visiting musicians. Dancing was a good form of physical exercise for patients and at Powick Asylum in Worcester, a band was established in 1856 made up of asylum attendants. In his report for 1857, the asylum superintendent, Dr James Sherlock, wrote: 'The weekly amusements have been continued as heretofore, and with the same beneficial results. No other means of recreation have been observed capable of realising a similar curative influence and their value is enhanced by the large proportion of the Patients who can participate in them.'

In 1879, the 22-year-old Edward Elgar was appointed bandmaster of the band at the Powick Asylum. He had played violin at the institution for occasional orchestral concerts for two years before that. The band played music for the Friday night dances that were put on for the patients and Elgar composed a series of polkas and quadrilles for this purpose, now known as the Powick Asylum Music. This was his first professional conducting role and he kept the post for five years before resigning.

One patient at Powick who greatly enjoyed the weekly dances was George Colson, formerly a clerk from Dudley. First admitted in 1852 at the age of forty, he was diagnosed with monomania of pride. He had been in Droitwich Asylum for six years before that and had

Mentally ill patients dancing at a ball at Somerset County Asylum. Process print after a lithograph by K. Drake. (Wellcome Collection. CC BY)

numerous delusions about being Lord Dudley. According to his case notes, he wore white kid gloves at the asylum balls and danced 'with remarkable gravity of demeanour'. However, George did say 'very ungallant things to the females at times, though unintentionally'. He was a patient who could be 'trusted anywhere alone' and in 1882, he was allowed to attend the Worcester Races as a 'great treat'. George died in 1888 of senile degeneration, having spent almost forty-two years in lunatic asylums.

Patients could be visited by their friends or relatives on certain days of the week at specific times. Visits could only take place if the patient was not adversely affected by seeing these familiar faces. In the 1850s at the Buckinghamshire County Lunatic Asylum, the visiting hours were on Wednesdays and Saturdays from 10 till 5 o'clock. It was common practice in lunatic asylums for medical staff to screen letters written by patients to their loved ones, and vice versa, to prevent upset.

MEDICAL TREATMENT

In the nineteenth century, the 'humoral' theory of disease was also applied to mental illness. It was believed that excess yellow bile (choler) would overheat the system, and would cause mania or raving madness; conversely, surplus black bile (melancholia) would lead to dejection. This theory led to the frequent use of purgatives and laxatives to open the bowels of lunatic patients, which it was believed would rid the body of harmful excess toxins.

Drugs were prescribed for patients, particularly to calm them or to help them to sleep. This could include opium, chloral hydrate, morphine or potassium bromide. If lunatic patients were physically ill, they would be treated in the infirmary section of the asylum with similar drugs to those used in hospitals. Long-stay patients arguably had better care than being at home as every ailment was dealt with promptly.

RESTRAINT

At times, it was necessary to restrain mentally ill inmates who were a danger to themselves or others. Common restraints included coercion chairs in which patients were strapped, straitjackets to prevent movement of the arms, and leather straps to attach inmates to bedsteads.

From the 1830s, a new philosophy of non-restraint linked with moral therapy was introduced, largely due to the initiatives of Robert Gardiner Hill at the small Lincoln Asylum and John Conolly at the larger Middlesex Asylum at Hanwell. They abolished all forms of mechanical coercion, including straitjackets. Hill claimed that 'with a sufficient number of suitable attendants, restraint is never necessary, never justifiable, and always injurious in all cases of lunacy whatever!' The *Penny Magazine* (1839) described the principles of the regime at Lincoln as 'gentleness rather than force, the blessed influences of the bright sunshine and the balmy air rather than medicines and solitary confinement, cheerful and affectionate patience rather than whips and chains'.

In order to carry out these principles, both asylums had to appoint more keepers who were experienced in their roles; this usually necessitated an increase in salary. According to Roy Porter, Hill and Conolly claimed that security could be maintained through 'surveillance by vigilant attendants and a regime of disciplined work and exercise designed to stimulate the mind, tire the body, and foster self-control'. At the Lincoln Asylum in 1834, 647 incidents had occurred that had required some form of manual restraint but four years later, there were none at all. What's more, this dramatic result had been achieved without any deaths or suicides.

Seclusion – being forcibly placed in a locked room – was used as an alternative to restraint for violent patients. In their report of 1844, the Lunacy Commissioners commented that 'great numbers of the superintendents of public, and of the proprietors of private Asylums throughout the country are fitting up and bringing into use solitary cells, and padded rooms for violent and unmanageable

Lunatics.' It noted that Lincoln was the only asylum where seclusion was not resorted to. The Commissioners saw seclusion as a valuable remedy 'for very short periods, in cases of paroxysms and of high excitement'.

In his article on seclusion, Leslie Topp quotes John Conolly's view that the great advantage of a padded room was to render 'both mechanical restraints and muscular force unnecessary for the control of even the most violent patients'. At Hanwell, padded rooms were prepared 'by a thick soft padding of coir ... enclosed in ticken, fastened to wooden frames, and affixed to the four walls of the

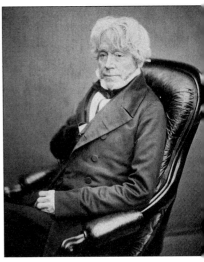

Doctor John Conolly. Photograph by Ma & Polyblank. (Wellcome Collection. CC B

room'. The window was guarded by a close wire-blind 'which admits light and air, but prevents access on the part of the patient to the glass or window frames'.

The Aberdeen Royal Lunatic Asylum operated a policy of minimal restraint, but in 1841 the medical officers pointed out that there were cases in which 'mild restraint is both judicious and humane', citing 'furious nymphomania' or the 'unbridled violence of an outrageous maniac'. The medical officers stated, 'We have no more hesitation in such cases, when other means have been useless, in applying the waist-belt, or the muff, than we would have in applying leeches or a blister against the will of the individual ...'

Every instance of restraint had to be recorded in a Register of Restraint and Seclusion. At the Surrey County Lunatic Asylum, restraint by seclusion or the confinement of patients to their own bedrooms was restricted to 'when they are under such excitement as leads to Quarrelling, Fighting, Breaking Windows, and to Indecent Conduct'. In 1848, sixteen male patients were secluded and five were restrained by mechanical means using a sleeve dress to prevent dressings being removed, bursting open the bedroom door and 'knocking his head against the brick wall of his bedroom'. In the same year, fifty-nine female patients were secluded whilst seventeen were restrained by mechanical means. This included one patient who was 'fastened to her bedstead by means of a soft belt round the waist, to hinder her from getting out of bed' for 365 nights. Other patients were fastened to chairs with soft wristbands to prevent them falling off; another spent forty-two days and nights in a sleeve dress 'to prevent her denuding herself' and a few violent patients were restrained to prevent injuring themselves.

In the last quarter of the nineteenth century, when many lunatic asylums expanded and became overcrowded with patients, it became more difficult to implement non-restraint and moral therapy policies. Seclusion with less restraint rather than non-restraint became more common.

RECOVERY

A good proportion of those who were sent to an asylum were deemed curable and could make a recovery after several months, or even years. Transfer between asylums could be of great benefit to patients during their treatment. In 1876, the physician at Edinburgh commented:

> In the cases of some patients, I think that a thorough change at a certain stage of recovery is most beneficial, and completes the cure, when nothing else would. It is a great pity that a ready transference of patients from one public Asylum to another for this purpose could not be more easily affected than is the case at present. I have often heard of sudden improvement in chronic lingering cases through removal to another institution, and have observed the same result to follow the transference here of such cases from other institutions.

If a patient was believed to have recovered from mental illness and was classed as convalescent, he or she would usually be released into the care of family or friends on a trial basis. This was sometimes referred to as being 'on licence' or 'on parole'. In some cases, especially for those whose health had improved but who had no family or friends to look after them, they might live permanently 'on parole' in the asylum. These patients had extra privileges such as being able to go out to the nearest town without an attendant.

Pauper lunatics were not discharged until the guardians of the relevant Poor Law union had agreed to it. Every union appointed a visiting committee to regularly visit the asylums that housed their lunatic poor. This enabled them to check on how many lunatics were chargeable to their union and to discuss each individual case with the asylum superintendent. If a pauper was deemed well enough to leave the asylum, he or she did not necessarily return to the workhouse. In many cases, such people were discharged to live with their family or friends who were subsidised to look after them.

Sadly, a relapse of mental illness was all too common for many patients. Those who were discharged from an asylum, particularly those of the labouring classes, found it difficult to procure employment. In 1841, the physician of the Aberdeen Asylum explained this was because 'Patients liberated from such an institution generally find the public prejudiced against them and doubtful of the validity of their recovery …' When coupled with 'the evils of idleness, poverty, and scanty diet', it was believed that 'no combination of circumstances could be contrived more likely to prove fruitful of secondary attacks'.

In many cases, patients preferred to stay in the safety of the asylum. In 1900, it was reported that six former patients at Aberdeen had voluntarily applied for admission to the asylum at the door. The patients were either 'labouring under morbid depression with the usual accompanying delusions, or were seeking the protection of the Asylum from imaginary tormentors'. The physician-superintendent argued that this proved former patients appreciated the value of the

The lodge gates at Prestwich Lunatic Asylum through which visitors entered, postmarked 1907. (Author's collection)

treatment at the asylum and would go to 'disprove the erroneous ideas and prejudices entertained by many of the general public' about the way asylums worked and how patients were treated.

Case Study: Ernest Jacob

When a patient was admitted to a lunatic asylum, it was not just their life that altered dramatically. His or her close family and friends were also deeply affected, especially when there were changes in the behaviour, personality and mood of their loved one.

Born in 1859, Ernest Jacob was the son of the co-founder of the Jacob biscuits business. He was a geologist, having qualified at the Royal School of Mines in London. In 1878, he travelled with his mother Hannah and sister Edith to New York (his father had drowned in an accident in 1861). In the US, Ernest worked for the US Geological Survey of the Rocky Mountains in Colorado.

Sometime after 1883, they returned to England and Ernest began to feel very melancholy, attempting suicide on a number of occasions. By May 1888, he was living with his mother and sister in a flat at 60 Wynnstay Gardens, Kensington; it's likely that it was from this mansion block that he jumped through a closed window some 50 feet from the ground. Ernest sustained a fractured spine and was attended by surgeon Stanley Boyd for nine weeks afterwards.

On 1 August 1888, Ernest became a patient at the York Retreat. Stanley Boyd was one of the medical professionals who signed the certificate declaring Ernest's insanity. Dr Boyd wrote that Ernest had explained his suicide attempt 'by saying that he wished his income to pass to a poor uncle in America in order that he (the uncle) might return to England & live with Mrs Jacob (the patient's mother). From his conversation since I know that Ernest Jacob's mind is bent on suicide.' He added: 'Ernest Jacob's mother (Mrs Jacob) tells me that Ernest Jacob persistently refuses to see his sister, believing that his so doing would in some way injure her.'

Daniel Hack Tuke was one of the best known and highly regarded psychiatrists of the nineteenth century, and his great-grandfather had founded the York Retreat. He also examined Ernest at 60 Wynnstay Gardens: 'He expects some dread event will happen to the world unless he prevents it by destroying himself. He has repeatedly asked me to end his life by morphine while I have attended him since he jumped through a window in May and continues to be intensely suicidal.' Ernest's sister Edith signed the Order for the Reception of a Private Patient and he was moved up to the Retreat in York. The cost of his 'lodging, maintenance and care' as well as 'wearing apparel and the repair of the same' was four guineas per week, and Ernest's mother Hannah signed an agreement to pay this.

In the admission register, Ernest was 'suffering from effects of injury to spine' and his diagnosis was melancholia. Under 'supposed cause', there was a question mark; no one could explain what had triggered Ernest's mental illness. In his case files, the medical officer wrote that 'at first sight [Ernest] seems to have very little the matter with him but when he begins to talk of death and suicide, he soon shows that he still retains his suicidal tendencies. He told me that he had jumped through a high window on purpose as he said that he was tired of his life.'

Ernest's delusions made him difficult to control, requiring an attendant day and night to watch over him. On 3 August, the medical officer wrote that he had found him 'in a very excited condition shouting at the top of his voice. Declared he was Jackson the murderer and had therefore but a short time to live. Would take no tea – said it was no good taking nourishment when he had to die.' It was quite common for someone with mental illness to have delusions about being someone with a high profile in the news. 'Jackson the murderer' was John Jackson, alias Charles Wood Firth, who killed a warder in May that year at Strangeways Prison before escaping and going on the run; he was captured in June and executed on 7 August.

On 6 August, Ernest was still refusing to open letters addressed to him as he said they could not be for him because his name was not Jacob. The following week, he started to refuse food and was fed by a tube; he also broke a bed pan by throwing it at the window when he said 'he saw the Devil'. In early September, he tried to rush for the window during the night but was stopped by the attendant.

By March 1889, Ernest was 'very much improved' and taking 'a keen interest in all around'. By May, he was 'much more cheerful' and gave a full account of his attempted suicide, 'which appears to have been unpremeditated & done on the impulse. He declares that his mother seemed to think him a burden to her, & so, out of pique he attempted his life. He acknowledges the folly & wickedness of self-destruction.'

In July 1889, he was 'very variable'. It was recorded that he was 'sometimes cheerful, enjoys life, goes in for his pursuits of collecting fossils, butterflies, birds' eggs etc., at other times he is despondent, given to fits of tears & despondency. His letters, considering his previous attainments, are childish & vacant.'

In November, there was the first intimation of fractured relationships with his family: 'He has a strange dislike of his mother & sister & states that he has no desire to see them again. He expresses no wish to go home & appears well & happy here. He writes, reads and otherwise occupies his mind, he is allowed to do much as he pleases.'

By 1 February 1890, Ernest was dining with the other patients and associating more with them but he was delusional about his sister and mother, declaring his sister to be 'immoral'. From 27 September to 4 October, Ernest was 'away on leave of absence for a fortnight, at Gainsborough House, Scarborough'. This was the seaside property that the Retreat leased for convalescent patients. Ernest 'was much benefited by the change'.

However, in January 1891, when the medical officer suggested he might think about leaving the Retreat, Ernest was 'very strange and abnormal in his ideas'. He had no wish to leave or ever to see his family again because it would be 'painful to him & them'. He appeared normal 'but for this fixed, strange delusion'.

Over the years, Ernest seemed to develop a phobia of women, 'refusing to go to any entertainments where there are ladies'. It's not clear if this was connected with his rejection of his mother and sister but it must have been extremely upsetting and painful for them. He also refused to leave the Lodge at the Retreat for any reason, not wanting to ever go on holiday to Scarborough again.

By 1909, the medical officer wrote that Ernest 'seems to have little idea of the value of money & if allowed would squander it recklessly'. Indeed, this was a facet of Ernest's behaviour that his sister Edith was particularly worried about. In letters she wrote to the doctors looking after him, she was concerned that if he ever left the Retreat, he would give all his money away.

In 1913, Ernest's mother Hannah died and he became Edith's responsibility. Although she often visited York, Ernest always refused to see her. Ernest had £1,000 invested in the biscuit company, which gave him approximately £42 per annum, plus income from property near Waterford in Ireland. As the years passed, Edith set up a trust so that Ernest's care could continue after her death; she died in 1938. Ernest remained a patient at the Retreat until he died in 1943, having spent almost fifty-five years in the asylum.

Sources: The Retreat Admission Papers (RET/6/1/9), Admission Register (RET/6/2/3/1), Casebook Males (RET/6/5/1/15), Casebook Males (RET/6/5/1/19); all at Borthwick Institute for Archives, University of York.

(With thanks to Walter Jenkins for this information about his ancestor, and to Borthwick Institute for Archives, University of York for permission to quote from Ernest Jacob's records.)

Chapter 6

THE MENTALLY ILL IN WORKHOUSES

Anyone found unable to manage their own affairs independently could be deemed to be mentally ill, and had to be looked after in an asylum, workhouse or private madhouse. In England and Wales, paupers came under the remit of the parish before 1834 and the Poor Law union afterwards. It was part of the workhouse medical officer's role to assess all those of unsound mind, but the high cost of care in an asylum meant that only unmanageable, suicidal or dangerous cases were sent; the 'harmless insane' such as idiots, imbeciles and epileptics remained in the workhouse. According to Norman Longmate in *The Workhouse*, it cost from 3s 6d to 4s per week to keep a lunatic in a workhouse whereas fees at the county pauper asylums were often more than ten shillings a week. The main reason for this disparity was because the Lunacy Commissioners insisted on higher standards than the Poor Law Commission.

However, waiting until mentally ill inmates were too difficult to manage before sending them to an asylum was usually detrimental to their health. In these cases, they would have passed the acute, curable stage and would now be deemed chronic and hopeless. When magistrates visited the private Droitwich Asylum in 1844, they discovered a large proportion of dirty patients, 'it being the custom of the neighbouring Unions to send Patients in a very bad state, after they have been kept in workhouses until their condition has become truly deplorable'.

Bakewell Union Workhouse, circa 1900. (Author's collection)

In cases of misdiagnosis, a sudden deterioration in mental state or a delay in sending a dangerous lunatic to an asylum, workhouse staff and other inmates could be subjected to extreme danger. In 1877 at the small union workhouse in Lampeter, Mary Luke Davies attempted to strangle the matron. Afterwards, she was certified as insane and taken to the Carmarthen Asylum.

After 1845, the Lunacy Commission held authority over all lunatics wherever they were maintained, including workhouses. Their highly detailed, independent reports written after their regular visits to each workhouse reveal the living conditions endured by the lunatics and how they were treated by the workhouse staff. Whilst the unions were not legally obliged to enforce the Lunacy Commission's recommendations, the Poor Law Commission, later the Local Government Board, tended to back up their suggestions. Even though the reports on the lunatics are so detailed, these inmates remained largely anonymous – very few are named.

'HARMLESS LUNATICS'

Under the Poor Law legislation of 1834, mentally ill paupers were not a separate group in the workhouse classification scheme and there was no specialist accommodation for them. This meant they were liable to be housed with physically sick patients or the elderly. Their quality of life depended to a large extent on how they were viewed by the workhouse medical officer. If they were considered to be non-medical cases, they were usually left in the care of untrained, unpaid pauper nurses and were not entitled to the extra rations the sick received. In 1867, a writer from *The Lancet* visited the Cardiff Workhouse Infirmary as part of the journal's self-appointed 'Sanitary Commission' investigation. He reported that the imbeciles led a life 'which would be like that of a vegetable were it not that they preserve the doubtful privilege of sensibility to pain and mental misery'.

Who were the 'harmless lunatics' who became long-term residents in workhouses? In 1847, the Lunacy Commissioners identified three categories of workhouse inmates with mental illness: defectives from birth; demented and fatuous; and deranged and disordered. Two years later, the Poor Law Commission declared that every inmate was either sane and should be treated as an ordinary pauper without a special diet or was insane and should be certified as a lunatic.

But the feeble-minded did not fall into either category and remained an anomaly. The problem was the majority of epileptics, imbeciles and senile dements required constant care and attention by day and night, but there were simply insufficient staff in union workhouses to provide it.

Facilities for them varied considerably across the country. At the small Lampeter Union Workhouse in 1900, where there were five inmates classed as imbeciles, the Visiting Commissioner in Lunacy was 'glad to find that the imbeciles all have flock beds above the straw mattresses' and that 'the patients are kindly treated and properly cared for'.

In most medium to large workhouses, however, the picture was not so rosy. Overcrowding in the imbecile and lunatic wards was common, leading to a severe lack of personal space for the paupers. This was mainly because the county asylums themselves were overstretched and had insufficient beds to meet demand. For example, Colney Hatch Asylum was opened in 1851 solely to cater for pauper patients from the London Poor Law unions. But as Norman Longmate points out, by 1867, it had 'turned down 3,800 applications, due to lack of vacant beds'.

Overcrowding in the imbecile wards was a major problem at the Dudley Union Workhouse in Worcestershire. In 1880, the Visiting Commissioner described the effect on the imbeciles:

> Dr Higgs the Medical Officer ... accompanied me through the Wards and ... evidently takes great interest in these patients. All were tranquil and orderly in behaviour notwithstanding the serious overcrowding but I observed some black eyes among the men the result of quarrels such as often happen among patients of this class who have insufficient day space. ...
>
> The beds are so close that they touch each other at the sides and the patients have to climb into and out of their beds over the bottom. Apart from the insufficient space it can be easily imagined how objectionable it must be for insane patients, many of whom are of dirty habits ... to sleep in beds actually touching each other at the sides.

The problem of overcrowding at Dudley was eventually resolved by converting the old schools into accommodation for the imbeciles.

Generally, lunatics and imbeciles had separate male and female day rooms and dormitories from the other inmates but at smaller workhouses, this segregation was not possible. According to Anne Digby in *Pauper Palaces*, in 1863, 'only four workhouses in Norfolk had separate lunatic wards, and a further five segregated the mentally deficient from the other paupers.'

Even in workhouses where the lunatics and imbeciles were properly separated, there was little to occupy the mind. The boredom and monotony felt by imbeciles in the workhouse was highlighted by a Visiting Commissioner to one union in 1889. He commented: 'in the men's yards I noticed some pigeons, which are much petted by the imbeciles and clearly afforded them some pleasure and these afflicted men, especially those who cannot be walked out, sadly need something to enliven the dull monotony of their lives.'

Wherever possible, it was recommended to give the lunatic inmates activities or work to occupy the mind, and to take them for regular walks in the workhouse grounds. In many Poor Law institutions, illustrated publications and cheap prints were put in the wards. At one workhouse on the advice of the Lunacy Commission, a musical box was bought for the female lunatics, which 'gives much pleasure to the women and is occasionally lent the men who are not well provided with means of either occupation or amusement'.

The Halifax Poor Law Infirmary, postmarked 1905. (Author's collection)

EPILEPTICS

Epileptics, or anyone suffering with fits from another cause, were placed with the imbeciles and lunatics in the workhouse, even though their mental state would usually have been sound and lucid.

In 'A Walk in a Workhouse', Charles Dickens described meeting one such epileptic in a London workhouse in 1850:

> In another room … six or eight noisy madwomen were gathered together, under the superintendence of one sane attendant. Among them was a girl of two or three and twenty, very prettily dressed, of most respectable appearance, and good manners, who had been brought in from the house where she had lived as a domestic servant (having, I suppose, no friends), on account of being subject to epileptic fits, and requiring to be removed under the influence of a very bad one. She was by no means of the same stuff, or the same breeding, or the same experience, or in the same state of mind, as those by whom she was surrounded; and she pathetically complained that the daily association and the nightly noise made her worse, and was driving her mad – which was perfectly evident.

Epileptic inmates posed a very specific problem in Poor Law institutions. As a result of the lack of paid attendants to look after these inmates, especially at night, countless lives were needlessly put at risk. As one Visiting Commissioner in Lunacy pointed out in 1891, 'epileptic patients are especially liable to death from suffocation caused by their turning on their faces in a fit, not necessarily severe, without making sufficient noise to attract the notice of any but a trained attendant specially watching the patients.'

In 1878 at the Dudley Union Workhouse, there was one paid male attendant with two sane pauper helpers by day and night. The female attendant only had one such helper by day, but a second helper slept in one of the two ward dormitories at night. This lack of paid medical staff mirrored the situation in the workhouse infirmaries.

In the majority of cases, the medical staff of workhouses did not attempt to treat imbeciles or idiots. However, in *Workhouse Children,*

Frank Crompton highlights the case of Henry Webb, a boy who was an 'idiot … from birth' due to inflammation of the brain, who was successfully treated by the workhouse medical officer at Kidderminster in 1840. The treatment was 'bleeding, placing him on a "low diet" and keeping him quiet'. The guardians were pleased that Henry's health had improved as they were spared the expense of sending him to a lunatic asylum, which they had previously considered.

LIVING CONDITIONS

Members of a Visiting Committee, made up of a group of guardians from the board of every union, would have regularly visited their lunatic poor in the county lunatic asylums. Such visits were often invaluable as they allowed an opportunity for guardians to talk with trained staff accustomed to providing a high standard of care for lunatics. The guardians could observe the lunatics at work and leisure and the superintendent of the lunatic asylum invariably offered suggestions and recommendations that they could then implement in the workhouse.

In 1867, a visit by members of the Visiting Committee of the Dudley Union to Powick Asylum near Worcester prompted the guardians to review the bedding and sleeping arrangements for the lunatic paupers at the workhouse: 'We recommend the Guardians to continue the use of Iron Bedsteads in the Dormitories at our Workhouse and to have a few made with sides to attach for the use of patients subject to fits. We also recommend that Flock Beds and Straw Mattresses about two inches thick be procured for each patient …'

In lunatic asylums, patients would have been employed in various workshops such as carpentry and shoemaking. However, it was simply not possible to provide such varied activities for lunatic inmates in the workhouse because of the lack of staff to supervise them. The women were usually involved in sewing, knitting, carrying out domestic duties and working in the laundry whilst the men were less well occupied.

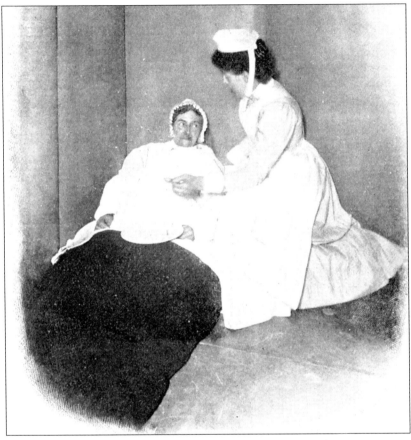

'Padded room' in 'Lunatic London'. (From Living London, *1902)*

In Poor Law unions, restraint could only be used when sanctioned by the medical officer and a record of each occasion had to be made in the Register of Mechanical Restraint. At one Poor Law union in 1896, a Visiting Commissioner disapproved of the restraint jacket being used there because it was 'of a type that we do not permit fastened by numerous leather bands and buckles. Proper light canvass [*sic*] jackets with closed sleeves ends and tapes will have to be provided according with the recently published Commissioners'

Rules.' By their very nature, workhouses were not designed to accommodate the special needs of lunatics or imbeciles.

CONTRIBUTIONS FROM RELATIVES

Wherever possible, the families of lunatic paupers admitted to asylums were asked to contribute towards the cost of maintenance. In rare cases where paupers had money of their own, the guardians of Poor Law unions took steps to use the money to pay for their maintenance in the asylum. In March 1854, the guardians of Dudley Union Workhouse discovered that Eliza Neale, an inmate of the Powick Asylum in Worcester, had 'money in her own right in a Bank'. They decided that 'at least the interest of such money be appropriated towards repaying the parish the expense of her support in the Asylum'. It's not clear how long this money lasted but Eliza was still at the Powick Asylum when she died in February 1886, nearly thirty-two years later.

'Harmless' lunatics continued to be housed in union workhouses at the end of the nineteenth and beginning of the twentieth centuries, with little improvement in conditions. In most institutions, the weak-minded were employed in the laundry or in other domestic work. By 1906, there were 11,500 inmates officially classed as of 'unsound mind' in workhouses.

The workhouse system ended in 1930 when Boards of Guardians were abolished. Afterwards, many workhouses became Public Assistance Institutions and others were converted into hospitals when the NHS was founded in 1948.

Case Study: Alfred Chenneour

People with undiagnosed mental conditions could find themselves in the workhouse when they were unable to work, or in prison if they committed an offence because of their illnesses. This happened to Alfred Chenneour, a hawker born in Exeter in 1853. He was destined to spend time in all three Victorian institutions: the workhouse, the prison and the lunatic asylum.

In 1874, Alfred married Emily Edith Ada Cain (known as Ada) and they had three children together: Alice Maud, Alfred Tubal Cain and William. A family story goes that Alfred was adjusting the harness straps on his horse and it kicked him in the head. Alfred's mind was never the same afterwards and he started having epileptic fits.

Whatever the cause of his problems, it appears there were long periods when he was unable to work and he was in and out of Exeter City Workhouse; it's possible that he was admitted each time as a vagrant to the casual ward but the records have not survived to confirm this. The *Western Times* reported in June 1886 that Alfred, an inmate of the workhouse, was charged with 'using abusive and threatening language' towards William Mayes, another inmate, and Mr Newell, the master. In his defence, Alfred said he had been 'wrongfully accused of taking away a tobacco box belonging to Mr Mayes' and became 'a little excited'. The master stated that Alfred had been an inmate for the last four years and that 'he had given the officials a great deal of trouble'. Alfred was sentenced to seven days' imprisonment with hard labour.

Four years later, Alfred was in the news again. In September 1890, he was charged with absconding from the workhouse. After the Casual Poor Act of 1882, vagrants were required to be detained until nine o'clock on the second day after admission; they could be detained until the fourth day if it was his or her second application to the same Poor Law union within one month. Alfred had been admitted to the Exeter City Workhouse on 18 September and was entitled to be discharged on the morning of 22 September at nine o'clock. The porter testified that Alfred 'absconded from the workhouse two hours previous to the time he should have left the workhouse, without performing his allotted task, which was wood cutting'. It was alleged that Alfred had unlocked the gate and run out of the workhouse. In his defence, Alfred said that the gate was not locked and that he thought he was entitled to his discharge.

At this point in his testimony, Alfred 'began to shake and nearly fell down in the box'. The master stated that 'the defendant occasionally had fits when he became excited'; this is the first official record that Alfred was having epileptic fits. It was also confirmed that Alfred had escaped from the workhouse two or three years earlier by getting over the gate. The case was dismissed after Alfred promised he would not go to the workhouse again.

Although there are no further news reports about Alfred getting into trouble with the law, it's unlikely he was able to keep his promise to stay out of the workhouse. It's not clear whether any members of his family were also inmates because in 1881 and 1891, Alfred's wife Ada and their children were living with her parents in Coombe Street, Exeter.

On 4 August 1899, Alfred was admitted to Exeter Asylum from the workhouse. The medical certificate stated that he had numerous delusions, some of which were connected with electricity, and 'he fits and excites and is dangerous then to others, he is daily getting worse in his mind.' The master of the workhouse confirmed that Alfred was dangerous to the other inmates. This was said to be his first attack of mental illness, which had lasted fourteen days; the diagnosis was dementia, partly caused by epilepsy. At the time, he was forty-two years old.

Alfred's mental state on admission was recorded as possessing 'numerous delusions, and says that he is only 21 years of age and he was married before he was three years old'. In addition, Alfred talked incoherently, 'wandering in and out of conversation'. By 4 September, his fits were not quite as frequent but he 'still fancies he feels electric wires working on him'. In January 1900, the medical officer wrote that Alfred was 'continuously unsociable, seldom speaks to his fellows, at times is antagonistic and excitable'. By May, Alfred would 'not occupy his time in any manner' and sat idly 'looking straight before him and is unstable if spoken to'. In October, Alfred was 'complaining and threatening', not being able to realise his position or to appreciate his memory was defective.

There was no improvement in Alfred's state of mind and he continued to be unsociable and apathetic, except after a fit, when he was 'excitable and abusive'. By 1905, Alfred was having frequent 'abusive rants' and his delusions about electricity became more prominent, making him 'homicidal at times'. According to the medical officer, after a fit Alfred was a 'dangerous and abusive patient'. This is why he remained in the asylum, rather than being looked after in a workhouse as a 'harmless lunatic' with dementia.

In 1907, Alfred would smile 'vacantly if addressed but never speaks'. He was still idle and unsociable but clean in his habits and 'very violent and quarrelsome in excitation with fits'; he was still experiencing the same delusions of 'electric persecution'. In August 1909, Alfred's heart started to fail and he died on 1 October, more than ten years after he was admitted to the asylum; he was fifty-two years old.

Sources: Exeter City Asylum Casebook Males (4034A/UH/2/3) and Casebook Males – Chronic Cases (4034A/UH/2/6); at Devon Archives and Local Studies Service, Exeter.

(With thanks to Pete Houghton for this information about his great-grandfather and to Devon Archives and Local Studies Service for permission to quote from Alfred Chenneour's records.)

Chapter 7

CRIMINAL LUNATICS

In May 1800, ex-soldier James Hadfield attempted to shoot King George III at the Theatre Royal in Drury Lane. Hadfield was insane as a result of his traumatic experiences in the French Revolutionary Wars and subsequent religious fervour in a cult, but he represented a dilemma to the authorities. As Mark Stevens points out in *Broadmoor Revealed*, historically, the verdict of not guilty by reason of insanity was 'reserved for those described as "brutes" or "infants", who were either unable to experience a solitary lucid moment or incapable of caring for themselves'. In these cases, insane prisoners were usually discharged into the care of relatives or to Bethlem.

Hadfield, however, had periods of lucidity and could function well in society, but he was still a dangerous lunatic. Clearly, he could not simply be discharged into the community. Hadfield was charged with treason and this meant he was granted a right to counsel, unlike other defendants at the time. His trial and the subsequent collapse of the case led to the passing of the Criminal Lunatics Act later that year. Under this landmark piece of legislation, Hadfield was labelled a 'criminal lunatic' and he was detained until 'His Majesty's pleasure be known'; this legal phrase effectively meant an indefinite sentence. Hadfield was to remain at Bethlem until he died in 1841.

In 1807, the Select Committee of the House of Commons had recommended that a national asylum for criminal lunatics be built. Instead, in 1810, when it became clear that Bethlem was planning a new building at St George's Fields, the government proposed that secure accommodation for criminal lunatics be provided there. The state would pay for the construction of two wings, one for males and one for females, as well as the medical care and maintenance of patients. The physician at Bethlem would remain in charge of the day-to-day running of the wards.

The two new wings for sixty criminal lunatics at Bethlem finally opened in 1816 and became known as the State Criminal Lunatic Asylum. These quarters were enlarged in 1838 when Bethlem itself was extended. According to Catherine Arnold in *Bedlam: London and its Mad*, the criminal wings were 'particularly grim'. They were two 'forbidding blocks' consisting of 'dismal arched corridors, feebly lit at either end by a single window in double irons, and divided in the middle by gratings'. Overcrowding was a major problem and the only pastimes were knitting, reading and running in the exercise yard, as well as playing the game of fives.

By the 1840s, these wings were full and from 1850, harmless criminal lunatics were accommodated in special wards at Fisherton House Asylum in Salisbury and at other asylums and prisons. Fisherton House stopped accepting criminal lunatics after 1872.

In 1853, William Hood, the new medical superintendent at Bethlem, was able to banish overcrowding by moving forty refined and orderly male criminal lunatics into the main building. A library was also provided. Afterwards, the criminal wing was described in *Old and New London* as being 'as cheerful as the other portions of the hospital' with an aviary, plants and flowers.

BROADMOOR

It was not until 1863 that Broadmoor Criminal Lunatic Asylum in Berkshire was opened; this was the first purpose-built asylum for the criminally insane in the UK. The first patients were ninety-five females and the male section of the asylum opened the following year. The majority of the criminally insane patients at Bethlem were transferred to Broadmoor, but a small number were retained. The patients at Broadmoor were most likely to have committed the most serious crime of murder.

Asylum for Criminal Lunatics, Broadmoor, Sandhurst, Berkshire. (Illustrated London News, *24 August 1867*)

In 1867, *The Illustrated London News* noted:

Many of the patients are employed, when in a fit condition, in various work about the garden and farm, in the wards, laundries, kitchen, and store-room, or in the tailors', shoemakers', carpenters', and other such workshops. There are classes for the elementary instruction of such as have not learned to read and write, with a good library for those who have; a billiard-table, with chess, draughts, bagatelle, cards, dominoes, croquet, and bowls for their amusement; besides music and occasional theatrical entertainments. A small number of the patients are voluntary attendants at religious worship in the chapel. ...

The situation is one of the most convenient for the purpose that could have been chosen within a moderate distance of London. The buildings ... were planned in isolated blocks, with a view to the more effectual separation of different classes of patients; and one block was built of great strength, like a prison, for the special security of violent and dangerous men.

Although it had been recommended as early as 1879, it was not until 1897 that feeble-minded convicts began to be segregated at Parkhurst Prison on the Isle of Wight. These were men and women who did not require treatment in an asylum but whose imprisonment in a standard convict prison was inappropriate.

DIAGNOSING INSANITY

The identification of the truly insane depended on the skill of the prison medical officer in making a correct diagnosis. It was his duty to examine all remanded prisoners to check they were free from any infectious disease, and 'in sufficient bodily health to take their trials'. For example, in 1874, the surgeon of the Salford Hundred County Prison certified that 36-year-old Abraham Royle, charged with unlawful wounding, and 58-year-old Ann Fielding, charged with unlawfully attempting to commit suicide, were of unsound mind and not fit to plead. Both were sent to Prestwich Asylum. Abraham died there at the end of the year whilst Ann was a patient for twelve years before her death.

Some prisoners were clearly insane, making a diagnosis straightforward, but the majority of prisoners with suspected insanity were more difficult to diagnose. This was compounded by the time constraints faced by the medical officer in examining the large numbers of prisoners in his care. When compared with the time taken in an asylum to examine and make notes on a new patient, it is hardly surprising that misdiagnoses were regularly made by medical officers.

According to Sean McConville in *English Local Prisons 1860–1900*, the medical officer at Holloway 'had to examine between twenty and ninety newly received prisoners each working day' and worked from 9.30 am to 9.30 pm. By 1894, Holloway received between three and thirteen mental cases every day.

Dr David Nicolson, the Superintendent of Broadmoor Criminal Asylum, had served in convict prisons for over ten years. In 1895, he told Gladstone's Departmental Committee on Prisons that at

110

A day room for male patients at Broadmoor. (Illustrated London News, 24 August 1867)

Broadmoor, he took 'between an hour and two and a half hours' to interview a patient for a report. He believed it was unjust for a prison medical officer to be pushed by any pressure of time 'to slur that most particular kind of work over hurriedly …'

It was not just a lack of time that made diagnoses of lunacy difficult. Malingerers often tried to feign insanity, making the job even trickier. Prison medical officers rarely had any experience or training in treating or diagnosing mental illness. The consequences of a delayed diagnosis or complete misdiagnosis of lunacy could be catastrophic for the prisoner. For this reason, the Superintendent of Wakefield Asylum told the Gladstone Committee that prison medical officers would benefit greatly from spending six months attached to a large county asylum since, 'The difficulties of diagnosis are very great, and it is requisite that they should have very fair training in insanity.'

Official prison returns reveal the shocking statistic that during 1883, 621 people had been sent to prison 'under suspicion of insanity'. The Prison Commissioners continued to stress that prisons were unsuitable for people of unsound mind: 'a prison is not a proper place for persons such as these. The care and management of lunatics is claimed and admitted to require special experience, and those who are so affected require peculiar treatment, and it cannot be expected that such experience should be available in prisons, more particularly in the small prisons which forms the large majority.'

Even when the medical officer diagnosed a prisoner as insane, the magistrates could still refuse to grant the necessary certificate for removal to a lunatic asylum on the basis of cost. The situation improved slightly with the passing of the Criminal Lunatics Act of 1884, under which prisons could obtain certification for criminal lunatics and have them transferred to asylums. In order to reduce the number of refusals for certificates for criminal lunatics, maintenance charges were to be paid by the Treasury during the period of their prison sentence.

Despite the new legislation, insane people were still being sent to prison. From 1889 to 1890, ninety-three sentenced prisoners 'were found to be insane on reception'. In his report for 1893, Dr Robert Gover, the Medical Inspector of Prisons, referred to these insane prisoners: 'All were unfit for prison discipline, and many must have been unable to understand why they were placed upon their trial, or the meaning of any of the legal proceedings taken. The insanity was very obvious in most cases.'

Even though many prisoners and convicts had a history of mental illness and were known to the authorities, they still had to spend time in prison rather than be sent straight to an asylum. Thomas Futerill of Kempsey in Worcestershire was a serial offender. He had twice been convicted of felony before he was given his first sentence of penal servitude. In December 1853, after 'breaking and entering the dwelling-house of his father' and stealing a quantity of goods, which he pawned, Thomas was sentenced to six years' imprisonment with hard labour in a government-run prison. As a convict, he was sent to Millbank, where he would have undergone nine months' separate confinement before serving out the rest of his sentence at another prison.

On 11 December 1861, Thomas was in court again in Worcester. He was convicted of obtaining goods under false pretences and was sentenced to eight years' penal servitude. Two weeks later, there is the first indication that he was suffering with mental illness. On 26 December, he was sent to Powick Asylum, but by 18 January 1862, he was transferred to Bethlem. There he was diagnosed with 'melancholia subject to fits'. Two years later, in March 1864, Thomas was moved to Broadmoor. At some point, Thomas was granted his liberty on a 'ticket of leave', as long as he regularly reported to the police in Worcester.

On 6 January 1868, Thomas was committed to Worcester Prison from the Worcester City Police Court 'on suspicion of having obtained goods, under false pretences, from several tradesmen in the City'. He was remanded for examination until 25 January, but in the interim, an order was received from the Home Office directing his removal to Powick Asylum. This must have been because Thomas was known to the authorities as a criminal lunatic. He was admitted there on 25 January as he was being destructive in his cell at Worcester Prison. He was diagnosed with mania with epilepsy, although not long after admission he was said to have feigned an epileptic fit. On 12 February, Thomas was removed under a Secretary of State's warrant to Fisherton House Asylum.

The following year, he must have recovered from his illness because on 13 October 1869, he was being taken from Fisherton House back to Worcester Prison. When they had almost reached their destination, Thomas escaped from the officer who was accompanying him. After he was found later, he assaulted a police officer and was sentenced to a month's hard labour. It's not known what happened to him afterwards.

Case Study: Rebecca Bell

One of the most distressing mental illnesses in women was puerperal insanity, often sub-divided into puerperal mania or puerperal melancholia. In extreme cases, these conditions could lead to infanticide by the sufferer.

Born in Ireland in 1853, Rebecca Bell née Halpin was the daughter of Patrick Halpin and Anne Tarrant. Patrick was a private in the North Cork Militia who served in India. He appears to have married his daughters off as soon as they were of legal age, possibly because his wife died young.

Rebecca married Richard Bell, a soldier in the 2nd Battalion 25th (King's Own Borderers) Regiment at Foot, in Colombo, Ceylon (now Sri Lanka) in 1867. She was fourteen and he was about twenty-four. They had three children while overseas but sadly, none of them survived infancy. Their fourth child, Lucy Harriet, was born in September 1876 while Richard was serving as a colour sergeant with the 1st Royal Lancaster Militia.

In 1877, the couple were living at the Fulwood Barracks in Preston. On 7 August, tragedy struck. While Richard was away for a few days, Rebecca was found by the side of the canal, having drowned Lucy and tried to commit suicide herself; Lucy's body was found the day after. The *Lancaster Gazette* (15 August 1877) reported on the inquest in minute detail.

The first witness was Rebecca's husband. He stated: 'There was a strange appearance about my wife that caused me uneasiness and apprehension about the state of her mind, some three or four days before I left home. She complained of pains in her head, and her mind was very unsettled. In the midst of any employment she would start up suddenly and go and look for things which she had not lost, or did not want. I also noticed at times a vacant stare from her eyes. My wife has had four children,

*Rebecca Bell, who was found not guilty of murder 'on the grounds of insanity'
in 1877. (With thanks to Yvonne Spargo)*

which are now all dead. I first noticed her strange appearance in
May last, and she was attended by Dr. McCall, the regimental
doctor. In May she was insane for a space of thirty-six hours, when
she did not even notice me or the child.'

Rebecca's neighbour, Elizabeth Walters, confirmed that
Rebecca had been acting strangely since May: 'I was very intimate

with her, and saw a good deal of her. Ever since May last I have noticed an unusual appearance about her. I have seen her when she has been nursing her baby, put it down suddenly, put both of her hands to the side of her head, and say, "Oh, Mrs. Walters, my head." She was very fond of the baby, and has spoken to me about Lucy, and her fear it would die like the other three.'

Superintendent Pye saw Rebecca straight after she was brought to the police station at midnight. In her cell, he stated that 'she put both hands on the back of her head, and said, "Oh dear, my head." I said what is the matter, and she replied, "They are running knives and forks into it." She held it with her hands about a couple of minutes and repeated her former explanation. She then put her hands down and said, "I've drowned my child, and drowned myself, but could not. I feel I am in the way. I can't lay my husband's money to advantage same as other women. I can't put anything out. I've not been accustomed to keeping house." She then repeated, "I'm in the way, and I made up my mind for several days to drown myself and my child. I did not want it to be left behind to be knocked about by other people." Mrs Bell said that of her own free will, and without my putting a single question to her. The next morning, she asked if the child had been found, and appeared anxious that it should be found. She never asked if it was living.'

When Rebecca was brought from Lancaster Castle to attend the inquest herself, she said: 'I did not throw the child in; I jumped in with it in my arms. It was not the child I wanted to kill, but myself. I was out of my mind; I did not know what I was doing; my head was bad. I was so fond of her that I would not hurt her.' The jury returned a verdict of 'wilful murder' against her and she was committed for trial at the next Manchester Assizes.

The trial did not take place until 7 November, so Rebecca would have been held at the jail in Lancaster Castle for the two months prior. Again, the *Lancaster Gazette* (10 November) reported on the trial. An important witness was Dr McCall, the chief surgeon of the regiment, who was called in to see Rebecca on 25 May. He 'found her then suffering very severely, and said he had no hesitation in saying that on this occasion she was mentally deranged for a period of 50 or 60 hours. At that time she was so violent that it required two women and her husband to be constantly with her, as there was a fear she might do herself or her child some injury. Since that time he had cautioned her husband that she must not be left alone.'

The jury found Rebecca 'not guilty on the grounds of insanity' and she was ordered to be kept in strict custody until Her Majesty's pleasure be known. However, it was not until 7 May 1878 that she was transferred to Broadmoor from Lancaster Castle, when she was described as being of 'suicidal tendencies'. The delay in moving her from the prison to the asylum appears to have been because Rebecca's husband had no means to maintain her there. As Chorley was Rebecca's last legal place of settlement, the guardians of the Chorley Poor Law Union were ordered to pay fourteen shillings a week for her maintenance in Broadmoor.

Rebecca's husband wrote to her and to the Medical Superintendent of Broadmoor at the beginning of her incarceration but does not appear to have made contact at any time afterwards. He retired from the army in 1881 and died in 1898.

On admission to Broadmoor, Rebecca was described as 'a woman of somewhat gaunt aspect, who gives a connected account of her life as the wife of a soldier at various stations and for some years in India'. She showed 'no prominent signs of insanity'. By October, she was 'recovering from a prolonged attack of mania, during which she was very noisy violent, erotic and obscene in her conversation and conduct'. She was 'still incoherent and noisy but is able to be up although requiring considerable supervision. Breaks glass occasionally but does not tear up her clothes as she did formerly – takes her food well.'

After this, comments were only made in her casebook once a year. This was because, as noted in 1896, she had 'gone on well and steadily since 1883. Is industrious cheerful and rational.' For some time, Rebecca's sister Sophia had been trying to get her released and finally, on 11 January 1897, Rebecca was discharged into her care.

All went well until August 1900, when Rebecca was readmitted to Broadmoor. She had been well and happy living with her sister in Farnham, apart from a day or two a month when her period appeared and she became fretful. According to her sister, in the previous fortnight, she had been very nervous and 'asked to be sent back to the asylum'.

Rebecca's case notes record she was suffering from melancholia: 'She states that she has been well up until a fortnight ago although she always had a morbid dread that the neighbours would find out where she came from. She complains of flushes and giddiness. Felt very restless lately and was afraid something would happen, she does not know what. She thought she might lose her senses and wander away. Her periods have been irregular lately. She is 44 years old and her nervous system has evidently broken down again under stress of the menopause.'

Rebecca remained a patient at Broadmoor, giving no further cause for concern until her death of cancer in November 1905. Sophia and her family migrated to Australia in 1913. Rebecca's story was kept a secret in the family until recent times.

Sources: *Lancaster Gazette* and Broadmoor Casebooks (D/H14/D2/1/2/1 and D/H14/D2/1/2/2); at Berkshire Record Office.

(With thanks to Yvonne Spargo for this information about her great-great-grandaunt, and to Berkshire Record Office for permission to quote from Rebecca Bell's records.)

Chapter 8

ASYLUMS FOR IDIOTS AND IMBECILES

In Britain, there was no legal distinction between lunatics and idiots until after the 1886 Idiots Act. It was generally assumed that it was impossible to educate idiots or imbeciles because it was thought they had permanent learning disabilities.

It was in Europe where pioneering work was taking place to challenge and change this preconception. In the late 1830s, Professor Edouard Séguin, Director of the School for Idiots at the Paris Institute for Deaf Mutes, began to test a revolutionary theory. He believed that the intellectually disabled did not have diseased brains; instead, they had suffered from arrested mental development before, or shortly after, birth. Using sensory training, Professor Séguin radically improved his patients' lives and in 1846, he wrote a seminal work about it entitled *Mental Treatment, Hygiene and Education of Idiots*.

Similar schools for training idiots were opened in the 1840s by Professor Guggenbühl in Switzerland, Professor Saegert in Germany and Dr Howe in the USA. Soon after, philanthropists such as Reverend Andrew Reed sought to improve the treatment and condition of idiots and imbeciles in Britain.

A small, privately run institution for feeble-minded children was opened in 1846 by Charlotte White in Bath; this was the first in Britain. In 1847, Reverend Andrew Reed established the first large-scale charitable Asylum for Idiots at Park House, Highgate, London.

The Royal Albert Asylum, circa 1900. (Author's collection)

A year later, there were fifty patients and by 1849, the number had increased to 145; demand was so high that a second branch was opened at Essex Hall, Colchester that year. In 1855, patients from both institutions were transferred to the new, purpose-built Earlswood Asylum in Redhill, Surrey.

Three years later, Essex Hall became the Eastern Counties Idiot Asylum. Across Britain, charities founded similar regional asylums: the Western Counties Asylum, Starcross near Exeter (1864); the Midland Counties Asylum, Knowle in Warwickshire (1866) and the Northern Counties Asylum, Lancaster, later known as the Royal Albert (1868).

In Scotland, the Baldovan Asylum for Imbecile Children was established near Dundee in 1855. That same year, Dr David Brodie founded the small Edinburgh Idiot School in Gayfield Square. In 1862, he was appointed as the first medical superintendent of the Scottish National Institute for the Education of Imbecile Children at Larbert, near Falkirk, Stirlingshire.

In Ireland, the Stewart Institute for Idiots was founded in 1868 at Lucan Spa, County Dublin. It was the only dedicated Irish institution for the learning disabled until the early twentieth century.

In the 1870s, there were increasing concerns about sending idiots and imbeciles to county lunatic asylums where they could be adversely affected by association with the insane. To avoid this, the counties of Warwickshire, Northamptonshire and Hampshire built separate 'idiot' wards at their lunatic asylums. The only other state-funded institutions for idiots and imbeciles were provided through the Metropolitan Asylums Board. It opened the Imbeciles Asylum, Leavesden and the Metropolitan Imbecile Asylum, Caterham in 1870; these were followed by Darenth Asylum and Schools in Dartford, Kent in 1878. The 1886 Idiots Act provided separately for idiots and imbeciles in order to better address their educational needs; as a result, Poor Law unions were encouraged to send some of their idiot inmates to the specialist charitable asylums.

ADMISSION TO THE ASYLUMS

The charitable idiot asylums catered for the industrious working classes, although the children of the wealthy were also accepted; at the Royal Albert Asylum, the fees were as much as 200 guineas per annum for private patients.

Parents who could not afford the fees had to subject themselves to the twice-yearly election at which the institution's subscribers voted for applicants. In June 1884, the parents of candidates for the Royal Albert Asylum included 'the widow of a National schoolmaster left with three children, one a cripple besides her idiot boy, lets lodgings for their living; a labourer with four motherless children to keep and care for; and a charwoman, with three children, whose husband has deserted her'. In each case, their difficulties were magnified by the problems associated with bringing up an imbecile child. Sadly, there were always far more applicants than places available. At that election, there were 107 candidates for fifty places, leaving fifty-seven to be bitterly disappointed. Where payment was possible, parents were encouraged to contribute something to support their child and to keep up 'a sense of responsibility and interest in their hearts'.

The asylums provided education and training so that on leaving, the patients could follow useful occupations in society. The children were usually aged from five or six up to fifteen and stayed for a period of five to seven years. There was, however, discretion to accommodate older patients for longer in special circumstances. Although the children had to live away from home, the idiot asylums offered hope to their families. Unfortunately, epileptic or paralytic children could not be admitted because of 'the dismay occasioned to children of weak intellect by the sight of one falling into a fit'.

DAILY LIFE

Kindness and patience were at the heart of the charitable asylums. Attendants looked after the children on a daily basis and assisted the teachers. Children were encouraged to keep in touch with their parents by writing letters, receiving visits from family members, and going home for short breaks.

Just as Edouard Séguin had demonstrated in Paris, the teaching was designed to awaken the dormant senses and feeble muscles. The resident physician at the Earlswood Asylum explained how a connection was first made with each child:

> The craving for affection is the chief characteristic of idiots and imbeciles. ... For the first month, we do not teach them anything at all, but simply try to attach them to us. ... When we have won his heart, we try to gain his head, and begin, slowly and gradually, to instruct him in the very simplest of educational subjects. ... Playfully the child learns to know, and then to write its letters; presently it puts them together and spells short words, and thus, step by step, we lead them on till the majority can not only read and write, but are also able to understand what they read or write.

The schoolwork was designed to be practical and engaging, and included learning how to tell the time and 'object' lessons to develop language and drawing skills. Perhaps the most popular was the 'shop' lesson in which pupils role-played buying and selling food items such as tea and sago, learning how to weigh things, paying with the correct coins and giving the right change. The children's training included gymnastics, drill, singing, music and outdoor exercise, as well as entertainments and occasional outings. According to the Royal Albert Asylum's medical superintendent, the aim was to 'discover, to draw out, and to develop any faculty possessed by their defective intelligences'. Music was such a great part of the children's training that 'almost all the attendants are required to play on some instrument; and concerts are got up weekly, often by the resident staff alone, with the aid of their imbecile patients.'

The success of the asylums was frequently reported to encourage donations and subscriptions, as at Earlswood in 1852:

> Amongst those placed under the care of the board from the commencement [in 1847], there have been 25 unable to walk, 114 unable to feed, dress, or take care of their person, 20 epileptic, 12 paralysed, 68 dumb, and 25 under nine years of age. … Six have been taught to walk, and 14 much improved who had a crippled use of their limbs; 27 who were dumb, or made strange and unmeaning noises, are getting the use of articulate sounds, and are beginning to speak; 48 have been taught to feed and dress themselves, and to observe cleanly habits; 23 have been taught to read, 27 to write, 11 to cipher, 16 to draw. Some are taught music – nearly all singing; nearly all are in the drilling or gymnastic classes; 90 can attend with propriety on domestic, and about 50 can attend on public worship and have pleasure in so doing.

As the children grew up, they were taught useful occupations. At the Royal Albert in 1885, 172 boys were employed in gardening, weeding

The Imbeciles Asylum at Leavesden, circa 1900. (Author's collection)

and farm work. Ninety-six of the girls were able to carry out bed-making, general housework, laundry work and sewing.

Case Study: Henry Isatte Freemantle

The patients at Earlswood Asylum for Idiots generally fell into three different classes: those who were elected by charitable subscribers and paid nothing; those whose families could afford to partly pay fees and were admitted at a reduced rate; and those whose families were prosperous enough to be able to pay the whole sum.

Henry Isatte Freemantle was admitted to Earlswood in September 1860 when he was twelve years old. In the register of patients, his class is recorded as 'private', indicating that his family paid for his fees. His father, also called Henry, was a professor of music in Sheffield and had been a lay vicar. Earlswood was a long way from Sheffield and Henry's parents only had one other child. To send him so far from home, they must have believed that it was the best place for him to develop mentally and to increase his skills.

Numerous details about each child's abilities and intellect were noted down on admission. Henry knew his letters, had a good memory and imitation, was fond of music and was very affectionate. His habits were 'correct' and he had good sight, hearing and taste, with normal smell and touch functions. Henry could also walk and run but could only partially dress and take care of himself. He was nervous but his chief problem appears to have been his speech, which was described as 'very defective'.

The casebook entry for Henry also notes that his parents were healthy and none of their other children were affected. Under 'general appearance', Henry's head was described as 'sugar loaf' shaped but his body was well formed. The medical officer recorded that he was a 'congenital idiot' although Henry's mother attributed her son's problems to an incident that happened while his father was playing in a performance.

The register also states that Henry was to spend half his time in school and half in 'picking class'. The patients at Earlswood were taught trades such as shoemaking and tailoring but those who were incapable of such skills picked materials such as wool and coconut fibre required for mat-making.

Henry's case notes reveal what he was learning and how he was getting on with various tasks. There are no notes for 1860 or 1861, but in December 1862, Henry had 'improved in speaking, also in drawing'. He could also 'tell the hours on the clock' and he knew 'all the coins, weights & colours'.

By January 1863, Henry could 'say me in two sounds' and by May, he could make 'himself understood in reading, spells all words but can say what very few of them spell'. He could also 'write in copy book text hand'.

In April the following year, Henry was described as 'much improved in every respect, counts to 27, knows all the coins, weights & measures'. By July, there is the first indication that Henry had epilepsy with the note 'fits as usual, healthy'. His admission notes do not mention he was epileptic so it must be assumed he developed the condition afterwards. In 1865, there was still 'general improvement' and the following year, his fits were 'not so frequent'.

Henry discontinued school in December 1867; he would now have been nineteen. By 1869, it was recorded that Henry went to picking class 'when well enough' but that the fits were now averaging eight per day.

In March 1870, Henry was having an average of six fits a day and 'was not active as formerly'. There was no improvement mentally. Sadly, on 25 May that year, Henry died; the cause was attributed to 'exhaustion from epilepsy'. He was just twenty-two years old.

Sources: Earlswood Hospital Register of Patients (SHC ref. 392/11/1/1); Male Casebook Recording Patients Admitted in 'General Register I' (SHC ref. 392/11/4/7); Duplicated Male Casebook (SHC ref. 392/11/4/14); Register of Discharges and Deaths (SHC ref. 6817/3/2/7); all at Surrey History Centre.

(With thanks to Sylvia Singleton for this information about her ancestor and to Surrey History Centre for permission to quote from Henry Isatte Freemantle's records.)

LEAVING THE ASYLUM

When children left the idiot asylums, about a quarter could work well under supervision and another quarter did well at home. Sadly, around half drifted into the lunatic asylum or workhouse system in adulthood.

The number of places provided by the charitable asylums was very small compared with the demand, mainly because there was no state funding and charities were dependent on subscriptions and donations. For example, in 1871, there were 29,452 people in England and Wales recorded as idiots or imbeciles, but only 3,456 were in specialist asylums. At the same time, there were 4,621 imbeciles in Scotland. Ten years earlier in Ireland, the census identified 7,033 people with mental disabilities. In 1881, the Royal Albert Asylum accommodated 2,422 idiots, yet there were 8,764 idiots and imbeciles in the seven northern counties covered by the institution. This meant that most learning disabled children in the nineteenth century were never given the opportunity of mental development.

'Imbecility' patient at West Riding Lunatic Asylum. (Wellcome Collection. CC BY)

Case Study: Emma Braeger

The Metropolitan Asylums Board provided accommodation for adult imbeciles from the London area at the state-run asylums in Leavesden in Hertfordshire; Darenth, Dartford in Kent; and Caterham in Surrey. In many ways, Emma Braeger was a typical imbecile patient. Born in 1878 in Bethnal Green, she was one of thirteen children; her father Joseph worked as a mineral water bottler. Emma had struggled at school and found it difficult to keep a place in domestic service; more worryingly for her family, she was impulsive and prone to outbursts of temper when upset.

In 1898, Emma fell pregnant after frequently leaving home and getting into 'bad company'. Sadly, the child did not live. According to the inquest that followed, Emma was taken ill in the street on 1 April 1899, was placed on a costermonger's barrow and taken to the infirmary, but her daughter Emma was born on the way and died before medical assistance could be obtained. The cause of death was 'suffocation due to accidental want of attention at birth'.

Emma was admitted to the Caterham Asylum for adult imbeciles on 3 June 1901 at the age of twenty-three. For the previous six weeks, she had been receiving treatment in the workhouse infirmary but clearly, she had become unmanageable. The certificate stated she was 'strange in her manner, very demented at times but has lucid intervals, She has fits of uncontrollable temper, at times. Acts strangely. Gets out of bed in her night dress and hides away from Nurse if possible.' Emma was the subject of imbecility, being very simple and weak-minded.

In August 1901, it was reported that Emma was 'very flighty and inclined to make mischief among the patients – sometimes sullen, impulsive and uses very bad language'. By February 1902, Emma was showing 'violent outbursts of temper and requires to be confined in a single room at these times'. In March 1903, although Emma was still flighty, she was able to control herself better and worked well. She was soon able to work in the matron's house and gave no trouble. Emma was discharged from Caterham on 8 May 1903 after almost two years 'to the care of her friends as improved'.

The following summer, in July 1904, Emma experienced her second attack of mental illness. At the time, she was eight months' pregnant so it's likely that she was admitted to the Whitechapel Union Infirmary at Vallance Road. This was where her son William was born in August that year.

Not long afterwards, Emma was admitted to Darenth Asylum for Imbeciles. Her son remained at the Whitechapel Union Infirmary and died in October at just two months old of 'marasmus' or failure to thrive from malnutrition.

Almost two years later, on 17 September 1906, Emma was transferred from Darenth to Bexley Asylum. Bexley was a lunatic asylum not specifically for imbeciles, so the authorities at Darenth must have believed Emma's imbecility had developed into something more serious. According to one of the nurses at Darenth, Emma had 'on two occasions attempted suicide. She was first admitted as an imbecile patient but has at intervals become extremely violent & suffers from delusions.'

On admission to Bexley, Emma's memory was much

impaired. She was simple and deficient in intelligence and education, but 'anxious to work & be useful'. Emma admitted 'attempting her life being violent & having a nasty temper. She looks nervous & timid but is not wholly irrational except as regards the delusions regarding attendants being against her.' She was 'quite certain the head nurse at Darenth was her personal enemy & made the nurses turn against her'. The original cause was thought by her relatives and friends to be the birth of Emma's first child but the diagnosis at Bexley was still imbecility.

On 22 September, the medical officer wrote that Emma's manner was that of 'a girl of 12' and noted she had been in a number of 'Homes and Imbecile Institutions'. He warned: 'She requires tactful management, otherwise she becomes … violent & threatens suicide.'

Three days later, Emma 'smashed a plate and threw her dinner on the floor' having been separated from another patient with whom she was 'shouting, laughing & disturbing the other patients'. After apologising, Emma went back to the laundry to work. By October, she claimed she was 'much happier than at her previous institution'.

However, Emma could be a troublesome patient. In January 1907, the medical officer wrote that if she was upset, she 'has no control of herself' and was 'most insolent' to staff. In April, she refused to get out of bed and struggled with a nurse, 'pulling her hair & striking her'. By June, she had caused no real trouble recently and was working well in the laundry.

In January 1908, she was sent to a different ward to separate her from another patient and to give her 'continuous supervision owing to silly suicidal threats'. Two months later, she smashed a couple of windows after she was taken away from 'doing private work in the ward'.

In February 1909, Emma asked the medical officer 'to allow her to have a cold bath as she feels it would do her good'. There is no note of whether the bath had the desired effect. By

September, the medical officer wrote that Emma 'works in the ward half day & in the laundry half day. Is silly, fond of attention but can be managed with firmness.'

By March 1911, Emma had been 'well conducted lately & controls herself much better than formerly'. However, she was 'apt to imagine that people are anxious to insult or take a rise "out of her"'. She was still noisy and boisterous at times and easily influenced by other patients, but she was a good laundry worker.

As the years went by, there was no change in Emma's mental state. She was regularly transferred in and out of specific wards, D and E wards being for refractory patients. This was the pattern of Emma's life in the asylum: periods of good behaviour punctuated by episodes in which she was easily upset, becoming noisy, abusive and violent.

By July 1916, there is mention of Emma wanting to leave the asylum. The medical officer wrote, 'Says she done a thing she ought not to have done at Dartford, & consequently was sent here. At present feels very well & works in ward. Would like to go home.'

In February 1917, Emma stated that her married brother, who was a chef, 'would like to have her out where she would be looked after by his wife'. Emma was more stable and amenable now and the following year she was 'most anxious to get out, says her brother will take care of her'. This shows that Emma's family kept up contact with her while she was detained. However, there is no further mention of Emma leaving the asylum and she remained there until 1928, when she died of bronchopneumonia and chronic nephritis. Her father objected to a post-mortem being performed, perhaps indicating that he still regarded her as part of his family.

Sources: Caterham Casebook for Females (H23/SL/B/14/013) and Bexley Casebook '13' (Female) Continuation of Patients Admitted 1899–1909 (H65/B/10/036); all at London Metropolitan Archives, City of London.

(With thanks to Ann Vennard for this information about her great-aunt and to the Oxleas NHS Foundation Trust for permission to quote from Emma Braeger's Bexley records.)

Whilst patients with mental illnesses were gradually given greater freedoms in asylums, the 'feeble-minded' or 'mentally defective' were being placed under greater control. A Royal Commission on the Care and Control of the Feeble-Minded (1904–1908) estimated there were, apart from certified lunatics who were under restraint, 150,000 mentally defective persons, and no less than 66,000 who were considered to be 'urgently in need of provision, either in their own interest or for the public safety'. This was the controversial era of the debate on eugenics: the breeding of a pure population.

Although adopted in other countries, sterilisation of mental defectives to prevent breeding was rejected in Britain. Instead, under the terms of the 1913 Mental Deficiency Act, male and female adults and children with learning disabilities were to be kept separate and under control in state-run 'mental deficiency colonies'. The inmates included profoundly disabled 'idiots', imbeciles, and two types of feeble-minded: those who were mildly disabled but had some degree of independency, and the 'moral defectives', those who 'cannot distinguish right from wrong and represent a grave danger to the community'. Colonies housed between 900 and 1,500 people, separated out into a series of detached 'villas'. Under the 1913 legislation, there were also 5,000 imbeciles accommodated in a total of 106 certified institutions, certified houses and approved houses.

Under the 1927 Mental Deficiency Act, there was a new definition of mental defectiveness. It was defined as 'a condition of arrested or incomplete development of mind existing before the age of 18 years, whether arising from inherent causes or induced by disease or injury'. Cases of mental defect arising from encephalitis lethargica, epilepsy or other diseases came under the remit of the new legislation. The Board of Control emphasised their view that mental defect 'may exist in persons of some – or even considerable – intellectual capacity. The criterion, except in the case of feeble-minded children, is whether the individual is so mentally defective that he requires care, supervision and control.'

The idiot asylums continued to offer care and after 1948, they were absorbed into the NHS.

Chapter 9

MENTAL ILLNESS IN THE ARMED FORCES

Being traumatised by experiences during battle, receiving devastating news from home or being incapacitated by tertiary syphilis (general paralysis of the insane); these are just a few of the issues that could affect serving members of the Royal Navy and the British Army and lead to a breakdown in mental health.

If a mental disorder struck a man while serving at sea, it was the medical officer who would have tended to him in the sick quarters. If the voyage was lengthy, the agonies would have been prolonged for both the sufferer and those who were treating him.

The journals kept by the medical officers for each voyage reveal some disturbing cases. For example, James Oliver, a 32-year-old able seaman on the HMS *Seahorse*, was low spirited and melancholy so he was put in a straitjacket. He was placed on the sick list on 14 May 1797 and discharged on 19 May to Gibraltar.

Edmund Aikes, a landsman aged twenty-three on the HMS *Adventure*, was diagnosed with insanity, displaying 'a great deal of anxiety and melancholy without any apparent cause'. He was taken ill on 7 November 1799 and was discharged to sick quarters at Cowes the same day. The medical officer noted, 'this man had been on board eight months and would not sleep in a hammock but slept standing up or over a gun. Although Captain Mansel flogged him "on his posteriors once a week" he would not go to bed.'

On dry land, between 1755 and 1818, the Admiralty used

Hoxton House, a private madhouse in London, to accommodate its naval officers and men suffering with insanity. This was a very large madhouse and by 1815, there were 484 patients, of whom 136 were seamen or marines and sixteen were naval officers. The scale of this asylum led to adverse living conditions for the patients, with concerns being raised by the Inspectors of Naval Hospitals and other authorities.

Hoxton House subsequently became one of the madhouses that the Select Committee of the House of Commons looked into in 1815. They found that staff levels were extremely low, sometimes just one attendant for twenty patients. In six of the beds, patients had to share with another inmate. The dangerous were handcuffed and chained whilst violent and quiet patients mixed indiscriminately. Despite these highly objectionable conditions, naval lunatics remained at Hoxton House until 1818.

In that year, a section of the navy's Royal Hospital Haslar at Gosport near Portsmouth was set aside to form the Royal Naval Asylum. In its 1844 report, the Metropolitan Commissioners in Lunacy described this area of Haslar for the mentally afflicted as being 'admirably adapted to its purpose'. They commented: 'The rooms are lofty, spacious and airy; and they command a view of the entrance to Portsmouth harbour. There are excellent exercising-grounds between the Hospital and the shore, and the Patients are frequently taken out in boats.'

At Haslar, unmarried officers were required to give all of their half pay for their maintenance in the asylum; if they were married, half of their half pay was appropriated and the other half was paid to their families.

In 1863, the Yarmouth Naval Hospital became a naval lunatic asylum to take the pressure off Haslar, which was overcrowded. The building at Yarmouth was extended to accommodate thirty-seven new wards. One hundred and thirty lunatics were transferred there from Haslar and forty patients were moved from the Sussex County Asylum at Haywards Heath, where they had been boarded out.

The main provision for mentally ill naval personnel was still at Haslar and Yarmouth in the Edwardian period. A specialist psychiatric unit was created at Haslar where patients were assessed before being transferred to Yarmouth. Between the wars, a psychiatrist was employed at both sites.

ARMY LUNATICS

In 1819, a lunatic asylum for officers and soldiers was founded by the government at Fort Clarence, Rochester in Kent, 'it being found that military men, visited with insanity, were frequently unable to pay for such accommodation in private asylums, as their rank and associations required'. However, the site at Rochester 'was extremely prejudicial to the invalids, and prevented a proper curative process from being adopted'. In 1844, the patients were transferred to Shorncliffe Barracks, Sandgate in Kent as a temporary measure. The Yarmouth barracks (Yarmouth Naval Hospital) had been identified as a possible building that could be converted into a lunatic asylum for the army. After alterations were made, in October 1846, all the patients were transferred to Yarmouth in one day. They consisted of twenty-three officers, fifty-three soldiers and four women. There were also two medical officers, two ladies, thirty servants and soldiers, and twenty-three women and children. In 1849, mentally ill patients were transferred from the Royal Kilmainham Army Hospital in Ireland to Yarmouth.

Each officer had a separate room, comfortably fitted up with carpet and a French bed. They were divided into three classes, according to their mental condition, each of which messed together. The first sat down to table in the mess room, 'as comfortable as any gentlemen in private life, and with all the usual accompaniments of a regimental mess'. The second class were not allowed knives, only forks and spoons, while the third class had their meat cut for them and were only allowed spoons. There were extensive grounds for the officers as well as a terrace; there was also a spacious promenade room furnished with tables, benches, newspapers and books, and a billiard room with a billiard table and bagatelle board.

The men messed precisely as they did in their regular regiments. Each man had a separate bed with a hair mattress, and they had an airing ground, terrace and a promenade room to exercise. The women were placed in a distinct square from the men and also had their own airing ground and terrace.

The asylum was 'self-supporting' as the officers paid three shillings a day and clothed themselves whilst the men who were entitled to pensions had them appropriated to defray the expenses of their board and medical attendance.

According to the *Norfolk Chronicle* (8 May 1847), in the twenty-eight years the asylum had been in operation, 671 cases had been admitted. Of those, 193 were discharged 'cured', 155 were discharged 'improved', 241 died and eighty-two remained under the care of the asylum. The non-restraint system was implemented in the 1840s and in 1849, the Commissioners in Lunacy pronounced it to be 'one of the best-conducted establishments of the kind in England'.

In June 1854, the army lunatic patients were forced to leave Yarmouth when the Admiralty repossessed the hospital. Nineteen officers were sent to Coton Hill Asylum in Staffordshire, which had opened that year as an extension to the county asylum specifically for private patients. Sixty-nine soldiers and five women were transferred to Grove Hall Asylum at Bow, East London.

From 1856, a building at Fort Pitt, Chatham was used as an asylum for soldiers arriving from foreign stations who had been diagnosed with insanity. It could accommodate two officers and thirty-two men, but patients only stayed there for a short time while under observation. Afterwards, the 'quiet, industrious and harmless' were sent to their friends or parishes whilst the 'dangerous and helpless' were transferred to Grove Hall Asylum; an arrangement had been reached with its proprietor to accommodate the increasing number of mentally ill soldiers returning from the Crimean War.

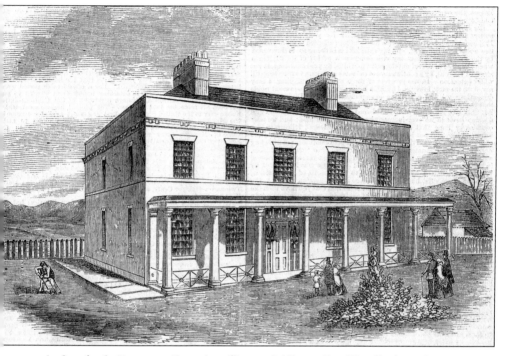

Asylum for the Temporary Reception of Insane Soldiers at Fort Pitt, Chatham, Kent.
(Illustrated London News, *21 March 1857*)

In 1870, the first purpose-built military asylum opened at the Royal Victoria Hospital, Netley in Hampshire; tucked away at the rear of the site, it was known as 'D' Block and became an important psychiatric hospital.

SHELL SHOCK

During the First World War, a new mental condition emerged: shell shock. Many soldiers and sailors in battle had a mental breakdown, experiencing a range of distressing symptoms including the inability to see, hear or speak, without any apparent physical injury; paralysis; insomnia; nightmares; and depression. Today, these symptoms would be attributed to post-traumatic stress disorder (PTSD).

According to the *Oxford English Dictionary*, the term 'shell shock' was first used in the *British Medical Journal* in January 1915 to describe a Belgian officer who 'presented practically complete loss of sensation in the lower extremities and much loss of sensation'; a shell had burst near him without injuring him physically. In February of the same year, Captain Charles S. Myers of the Royal Army Medical Corps wrote an article for *The Lancet* entitled 'A Contribution to the Study of Shell Shock', which detailed three cases admitted to the Duchess of Westminster's War Hospital in Le Touquet.

In the medical profession, shell shock was known as 'war neurosis' or 'war neurasthenia'. At first, it was not taken seriously, especially as many of the symptoms were similar to hysteria, which was a recognised condition before the war. Sufferers of shell shock were frequently suspected of malingering and cowardice. It's highly likely that many of the 306 soldiers who were court-martialled and shot at dawn for cowardice or desertion during the First World War were suffering from shell shock; these men were officially pardoned in 2006.

The majority of the mental cases that arose in the Expeditionary Forces during the First World War passed through 'D' Block at Netley. If a man was presumed to have a mental illness on the battlefield, he was admitted temporarily to the Field Ambulance and then transferred quickly to a Casualty Clearing Station or direct to a Base Mental Hospital. These were special Mental Divisions set apart from the other wards in the general hospitals. A medical officer with special psychiatric experience was in charge of each Mental Division; in France, they were at Boulogne, Le Tréport, Rouen and Havre.

Convoys of soldiers found to be psychotic were sent to 'D' Block at Netley via Southampton. The unit was run by Charles Stanford Read MD, and in his book *Military Psychiatry in Peace and War*, he described the process of receiving casualties.

'D' Block was purely a clearing hospital where cases were assessed. It had 124 beds, only three of which were for officers. The

The Cassel Hospital at Swaylands, Penshurst, founded in 1919 to treat shell shock victims. (Author's collection)

average stay was only five or six days before the casualty was transferred to another facility. If 'markedly psychotic', officers were sent to the Special Hospital for Officers at Latchmere, near Richmond in Surrey. For officers in 'the milder states and those only showing psychoneurotic symptoms', they were transferred to Lord Knutsford's Hospital in Kensington or the Maudsley Hospital in London.

Men were sent to one of the special mental wards, known as War Mental Hospitals, which had been set up at some of the war hospitals converted from county lunatic asylums. They were: The County of Middlesex, Napsbury (350 beds); Lord Derby's War Hospital, Warrington (1,000 beds); Welsh Metropolitan War Hospital, Cardiff (450 beds); Dykebar War Hospital, Paisley (500 beds); Auxiliary Hospital at Crookston (350 beds); Murthly War Hospital,

Murthly, Perth (380 beds); Northumberland War Hospital, Newcastle (100 beds); Notts County War Hospital, Nottingham (540 beds); Belfast War Hospital (500 beds); and Dublin War Hospital (300 beds).

Patients usually remained 'for twelve or nine months at the military hospital before being sent to institutional care under certificate, if such became necessary'. If an officer or man was admitted directly to a rate-funded asylum, he was classed as a 'private patient' and his maintenance would be paid by the Ministry of Pensions. Afterwards, he might then be classed as a 'Service patient' if it was proved that his mental illness was caused or aggravated by service during the war. 'Service patients' received extra privileges such as a special uniform distinct from the other patients' asylum dress and an additional allowance for cigarettes and other luxuries. They were also considered as private patients by the staff.

This arrangement also applied to 'non-pensionable cases' where the affliction was not attributed to military or naval service, but treatment was only to last until the end of the war and up to twelve months afterwards; these ex-servicemen were only eligible to be 'Service patients' if they had not been treated in an asylum before enlistment.

Shell shock was treated in a number of different ways, according to how each institution's psychiatrist viewed the condition. Violent electric shock treatment was used at the Queen's Hospital in London by Lewis Yealland to recondition the behaviour of patients, for example, to make those with mutism speak. This almost barbaric treatment was also used at other military hospitals. In Newton Abbot, Devon, at Seale Hayne Hospital, Arthur Hurst favoured suggestion and hypnotherapy combined with fresh air and physical exercise to 'cure' shell shock.

At the Maudsley, Major Frederick Mott maintained military discipline and offered quiet, rest and work therapy such as knitting and basket making. Psychotherapy, in which patients talked about their experiences, was pioneered at Maghull near Liverpool and at Craiglockhart War Hospital for Officers just outside Edinburgh; the latter was nicknamed 'Dottyville' by Siegfried Sassoon, one of its shell shock patients. Today, psychotherapy and work therapy are the cornerstones of treatment for sufferers of PTSD.

By the end of the war, more than 80,000 cases of shell shock had been treated by the British Army. Many more appeared in the decade after the conflict and according to John Stevenson in *British Society 1914–1945*, by 1928, there were forty-eight special mental hospitals still treating 65,000 victims of shell shock.

In the Second World War, psychological tests were used when recruiting officers and there was a greater awareness and understanding by the Army Medical Services about the mental toll the stresses of warfare could take on individuals.

Case Study: Harold Tuckey

The effects of shell shock on members of the armed forces could last for decades, long after the original battle or war had ended. For Harold Tuckey, it was to blight his life and lead to long periods of hospitalisation for mental illness.

Harold Tuckey who was admitted to Burntwood County Asylum in 1919. *(From Burntwood County Asylum Male Case Notes (D5456/C/2/20b) at Staffordshire Record Office)*

Born in August 1898 in West Bromwich, Staffordshire, Harold was the eldest son of Benjamin and Sarah Ann Tuckey; the couple had five children altogether. Benjamin Tuckey worked as an iron moulder and crane driver, but from 1909, he was also a part-time fireman at the Hill Top Sub-Station of West Bromwich Volunteer Fire Brigade.

In February 1916, Harold Tuckey went to work with his father at Hill Top and was appointed a volunteer fireman, aged just seventeen. He had joined the army by attesting in the Derby Scheme before his eighteenth birthday later that year and presumably chose to defer his service. The West Bromwich Fire Brigade personnel records reveal that Harold was 'called to the colours' in June 1917. He joined the 2/5 South Staffordshire Regiment as a private (No. 203849) but only his medal card has been found, showing he received the Victory and British medals. None of his service records have survived.

According to a report in the West Bromwich Free Press (4 January 1918), Harold's mother received intimation from the War Office that her son was 'an inmate of 10 General Hospital, Rouen, suffering from gun-shot wound and with the right leg amputated'. A family story goes that Harold was blown up on the Somme but it's more likely that he was wounded at the Battle of Cambrai in November/December 1918, in which the South Staffordshire Regiment was heavily involved. It was said to be this catastrophic event that caused his lifelong shell shock.

Having returned home and after a period of recuperation, Harold was reappointed as a 'permanent fireman' to the West Bromwich Fire Brigade at some point in 1919, working as a wireless operator. He then 'resigned through shell shock effects of the Great War, Sept. 1919'. This is the only documentation where the phrase 'shell shock' is used.

On 13 September 1919, Harold was admitted to Burntwood County Asylum in Staffordshire in the most extraordinary of circumstances. A newspaper report pasted into the admission register alludes to the reason, with the headline 'A Drama in the Moonlight: One-Legged Man with a Brick' and 'Shock Causes Death'. It appears that Harold had climbed on to the roof of West Bromwich Town Hall using a ladder left by a workman; he was wearing very few clothes and had smashed up his artificial leg. Sadly, the town hall caretaker, William Thomas Hutt, had a heart attack and died after the 'excitement' of hearing and seeing Harold on the roof and believing the town hall was under attack;

a verdict of 'death from natural causes' was recorded at the inquest.

According to the asylum admission register, Harold had had no previous attacks of mental illness and this may be why the medical officer did not attribute his symptoms to shell shock. Harold was usually good-tempered and his habits were temperate. He had been brought to the West Bromwich Infirmary by the police and the doctor there stated that he 'was lying in bed in a dazed condition unable to account for his actions except that he knew what he had done and that he had been compelled to act as he did and he hoped that he would be forgiven'. The night nurse at West Bromwich Infirmary added that he had been found 'in a nude condition on the roof of the Town Hall. He was unable to give any definite account of himself. He had pulled his artificial leg to pieces.' From that day onwards, Harold preferred to fold up his trouser leg and get around on crutches, instead of using an artificial leg.

On admission to Burntwood Asylum, Harold's diagnosis was Mania (II 8a), which stood for 'recent mania'. He was 'quiet but in a confused state' and 'able to talk sensibly and rationally'. Harold was in 'moderate bodily health & condition', weighing 8 stone at 5 ft 9½, and his heart and lungs were apparently healthy. He was classed as a 'service patient' as he was receiving an army pension.

The day after Harold was admitted to Burntwood, he was 'very exalted and self-assured in his manner ... whistling in a cheerful manner and impertinent and rude to the A.M.O. He soon quietened down and lapsed into a somewhat sullen state.'

Two days later, he was still confused 'and sometimes shows difficulty in recalling things to memory'. When explaining the escapade on the town hall roof, he gave as his reason 'the fact that he wanted to show people that there was still a war on!' Although Harold was quiet at night, he was only able to sleep for a few hours.

By 23 September, he was 'very dull' and he 'cannot be got to speak at times & at other times he replies briefly and in an abrupt manner to questions put to him'. Harold's behaviour appears to have alternated between dullness and being unwilling to speak, and being noisy and disruptive.

On 3 October 1919, the medical officer wrote that he 'continues to be very dull at times. At other times he shouts out and uses foul & threatening language towards imaginary people whom he apparently imagines are talking to him or about him or persecuting him in some way. He is too incoherent to get any intelligible statement from him, is sometimes noisy at night.'

After an eight-month stay at Burntwood, Harold was discharged 'recovered' on 10 May 1920. Sadly, this was not the end of his mental health problems. He returned home to live with his parents and four siblings, and he may have been manageable at first with so many people there to help out. However, family stories describe his behaviour as putting a strain on the household, especially for whichever brother had to share a bedroom with him. Harold was particularly noisy at night, as he had been for a time in the asylum.

The problems were exacerbated after Harold's siblings left home, one by one. In 1922, his older sister Marion got married, followed two years later by his younger sister Ethel. In 1929, Harold's father Benjamin died, leaving his mother Sarah Ann with her three sons at home. The following year, brother Percy got married.

Things must have come to a head again for Harold in April 1933 as he was admitted to Hallam Hospital, West Bromwich. Three years later, his mother Sarah Ann died after an operation at the same hospital; it's not known if Harold was allowed to visit her. Harold remained at Hallam until December 1937, when he was admitted once more to Burntwood Asylum. Clearly, he needed more specialist treatment than the hospital could give and he was to remain at the asylum until his death in 1941 from tuberculosis. The young man who had gone off to fight for king and country was scarred mentally and physically by his experiences, and was robbed of the chance of having a normal family life like his siblings. Few members of the next generation knew of his plight.

Sources: West Bromwich Fire Brigade Records of Staff (CB-B/12/2/1) at Sandwell Community History and Archives Service; Burntwood County Asylum Male Register (D5456/C/1/67) and Male Case Notes (D5456/C/2/20b) at Staffordshire Record Office.

(With thanks to Roy Tuckey and Carl Higgs for this information about their uncle and great-uncle, and to Staffordshire Record Office for permission to quote from Harold Tuckey's records up to 1919.)

Chapter 10

SOURCES

The first indication that you have an ancestor who spent time in a lunatic asylum may be from a family story told in hushed tones and passed down the generations. Such tales should always be taken with a pinch of salt until they can be proved or disproved by official sources, although there is often a grain of truth in them. There are a number of general sources and records specific to lunatic asylums that can be used to help you find out more.

THE CENSUS
Another clue may be found on the census when you unexpectedly find your forebear living in an institution, often miles away from their families. The census is an official count of the population, and the first one in Britain was taken on 10 March 1801; a census has been taken every ten years since, except 1941. Censuses are usually closed for 100 years, and the dates on which the currently available census returns were taken are 6 June 1841; 30 March 1851; 7 April 1861; 2 April 1871; 3 April 1881; 5 April 1891; 31 March 1901; and 2 April 1911. The 1921 census was taken on 19 June and is unlikely to be available to the public before 2022.

The first useful census for family historians is the one taken in 1841, as the previous returns were mainly for statistical purposes. However, this census does not provide as much information as those in later years because the ages of adults over fifteen were rounded down to the nearest five years, and places of birth were not given – simply an 'N' for no and 'Y' for yes in answer to the question 'Were you born in this county?'

Later census returns give the full address, the full name of the householder and everyone in the household (plus their relationship to the head of the house); their ages, condition as to marriage, place of birth and occupation; if blind, deaf or dumb, and later, if an idiot or lunatic.

On the census, each place was divided into a number of enumeration districts covered by individual enumerators, so unless you use an online search facility, you will need to know roughly where your ancestor was living.

Census returns for England and Wales 1841–1911 are freely available at The National Archives, and for specific areas at county record offices and large city libraries. Scottish census returns for the same years can be viewed on the ScotlandsPeople website using credits (www.scotlandspeoplehub.gov.uk/index) or at county record offices. For Ireland (including the counties that became Northern Ireland), you can search and view the census returns for 1901 and 1911 for free on The National Archives of Ireland census website (http://www.census.nationalarchives.ie/). You can also see census fragments and substitutes for 1821–1851.

Census returns can also be viewed on most commercial family history websites on a subscription or pay-per-view basis. Many archives and libraries subscribe to these websites so it is often possible to use the service for free. Another option is to use one of the various free genealogy websites. With digitised records, you can easily search the census by place or name, but be aware it is always possible that your ancestor's name was incorrectly transcribed, leading to a 'not found' scenario.

Such was the stigma associated with mental illness that many lunatic asylums did not give their patients' full names on the census, simply providing initials instead; this was particularly the case in 1861, when initials were all that were required by the authorities. The practice did vary with some asylums giving an initial and surname, whilst others provided full names. If you find a census entry where only initials are given, it is almost impossible to prove

The Denbigh Asylum, postmarked 1909. (Author's collection)

which one was your ancestor. The exception would be if he or she had an unusual place of birth or occupation, or if the patients' records have survived and you can match them up with the initials.

From the 1871 census, mental impairments were added to the medical disabilities column, asking whether anyone in the household was an 'imbecile or idiot' or a 'lunatic'. By 1901, 'lunatic' was still an option in the infirmity column but the word 'idiot' was replaced with 'imbecile feeble-minded'. This change was made because the census authorities suspected that cognitive impairments were being under-reported, partly because of a lack of understanding about the terms 'idiot' and 'imbecile' and partly because of the stigma associated with them. On the 1911 census, the mental conditions listed were 'lunatic' or 'imbecile or feeble-minded'. Householders were also asked to state the age at which a person became afflicted.

Bear in mind that although someone may be listed as a widow or widower on the census, it doesn't automatically mean their spouse was dead. It was not until the 1937 Divorce Act that it was legal to divorce someone who had become incurably insane. Before then, divorce had only been possible if it could be proved that someone was insane at the time they married. If a person wanted to keep secret the fact their husband or wife was in an asylum, claiming they were widowed was an easy way to do it.

THE 1939 REGISTER

To find out if your ancestor was still in a mental institution on the eve of the Second World War, check the 1939 Register. It can be viewed on several commercial family history websites on a pay-per-view or subscription basis. Originally kept for National Registration purposes, the register was a working document used for the National Health Service.

Column 5 of the register was left blank for households but completed for institutions like prisons and hospitals; lunatic asylums were known as mental hospitals after 1930. 'O', 'V', 'S', 'P' and 'I' were completed in the column to indicate whether a named individual was an officer, visitor, servant, patient or inmate. One would expect the mental hospitals to use the term 'patient' because it implies someone who was receiving some kind of treatment. However, there does not seem to have been definitive advice given to the institutions about whether to use 'patient' or 'inmate'. For example, Brighton and Barnsley Hall mental hospitals used 'patient', whilst Devon and Chester mental hospitals used 'inmate'.

Full names are given because the objective behind the register was to produce national registration cards. This is useful if you're not sure if an individual is actually your ancestor on previous censuses where only initials may have been given. The occupation listed is the one followed by each patient prior to admission; some mental hospitals make the distinction very clear by prefixing each occupation with the word 'formerly'. Sometimes, all you will see is the word 'incapacitated'. The gender is given, as is 'S', 'M', 'W' or 'D' for single, married, widowed or divorced. The hospital authorities were supposed to fill in the date and year of birth, but often only the year is given. If surnames are crossed out with a different name written above it, this was usually because the individual got married and changed her name, or got divorced and reverted back to her maiden name; the correction would have been made by the National Health Service authorities.

DEATH CERTIFICATES

If your ancestor died in a lunatic asylum or mental hospital, the death certificate can provide some interesting information about the circumstances of his or her demise. It was common for death certificates to record the addresses of institutions, rather than their names, to avoid the stigma of mental illness in Victorian society. Don't automatically discount a death that's miles away from where your ancestor lived. He or she could have been transferred to an asylum in another county.

You can order a PDF of a registered death in England or Wales for the period 1837–1957 from the General Register Office (https://www.gro.gov.uk/gro/content/certificates/); this costs less than a death certificate. PDFs were originally offered as a pilot for a limited period but the service has continued and there is currently no planned end date.

Starting in 1855, Scottish death certificates provide more information than English and Welsh versions, including the name, surname and rank or profession of the deceased's father plus the name and maiden surname of their mother. If you just need an unofficial copy of a certificate (also known as an extract) for your research, you can order it via ScotlandsPeople (www.scotlands people.gov.uk) using credits. Otherwise, you can order official certified paper copies of death certificates from the same source.

Copies of death certificates for Northern Ireland from 1864 can be ordered from the General Register Office of Northern Ireland (https://www.nidirect.gov.uk/services/go-groni-online); only death certificates that are over fifty years old can be purchased in this way.

NEWSPAPERS

If your ancestor got into trouble with the law as a result of mental illness, he or she might be mentioned in a local newspaper report. Attempted suicide was a crime until 1961, so there were often reports about court cases prosecuting those who failed in their attempts. There were also mentions of inquests on those who had committed suicide. Very rarely, your ancestor may be named in reports about conditions in a specific asylum.

Another reason your forebear may be in the news is if he or she was challenging being committed to an asylum and trying to prove their sanity. Newspaper reports may also be the only evidence you find relating to cases of contested wills after the death of a mentally ill person.

Historical local newspapers can be consulted at county record offices and local history libraries. Hundreds of titles can also be searched and viewed online via the British Newspaper Archive (http://www.britishnewspaperarchive.co.uk); these newspapers are also available on Find My Past to Pro subscribers (www.findmy past.co.uk). Some libraries also subscribe to British Library Newspapers (1800–1900) and The Times Digital Archive (1785–1985); you may be able to access these resources for free from home by logging in with your library card.

WILLS

If there was a delay in granting probate after the death of a person, it could be because the will was contested by the deceased's relatives. This may be because he or she was 'of unsound mind' at the time of making the will. Probate is a complicated area to research and there were different arrangements and documentation at different times for England and Wales, Scotland and Northern Ireland.

To find out more, read the relevant research guide for the country you're interested in. For England and Wales, see The National Archives guides on 'Wills or administrations before 1858' and 'Wills

Winter Entertainments at St Luke's Hospital. (Illustrated London News, *8 February 1862)*

or administrations after 1858' (http://www.nationalarchives.gov.uk/ help-with-your-research/research-guides/wills-or-administrations-after-1858/). For Scotland, look at the National Records of Scotland guide to 'Wills and Testaments' (https://www.nrscotland.gov.uk/ research/guides/wills-and-testaments). The Public Record Office of Northern Ireland's guide to 'Wills and Will Calendars' is also online (https://www.nidirect.gov.uk/articles/about-wills-and-will-calendars).

LUNATIC ASYLUM RECORDS
Most lunatic asylum records are held in local archives but remember that not all patients' documents have survived and there may be gaps in coverage. You can find out what's available by searching the

Hospital Records Database (www.nationalarchives.gov.uk/hospital records); this site is no longer updated but is an excellent reference source.

In Scotland, responsibility for hospital and asylum records fell to the Health Boards. These documents were sometimes merged into university archives; in other cases, records may be held by the Health Board Archives for the relevant area. Scottish Indexes has a useful directory of mental health institutions (https://www.scottishindexes .com/institutions/countylist.aspx). For each one, the location of the records is listed.

Most records for asylums in what is now Northern Ireland are held at the Public Record Office of Northern Ireland (https://www. nidirect.gov.uk/proni).

Generally speaking, you're more likely to find details of your ancestor if he or she was treated in a county pauper asylum rather than a private madhouse. That's because few records of private institutions have survived. The archives of some long-running private asylums such as Ticehurst and the York Retreat are notable exceptions.

The records for patients in asylums contain sensitive clinical information and are therefore closed to the public for 100 years under the terms of the Data Protection Act. This is designed to protect the privacy of the patients who may still be alive. Bear in mind that this rule usually applies to the date of the last entry in the register, which may be many years after your ancestor was in the institution. The only exception would be registers of deaths where it's clear that the individuals are already deceased and therefore Data Protection does not apply.

It is sometimes possible to gain access to closed medical records if you can prove the patient is deceased. To do this, you would need to make a formal request to the archive that holds the records, and the staff would ask you to seek permission from the copyright holder, usually the NHS Trust responsible for the asylum or mental hospital; some archives will do this on your behalf. As these registers are closed to the public, it is not usually possible for you to do your own research into the records. This is because information about other individuals who are named in the register will be visible to you and their identity and privacy has to be protected by law.

Archive staff can usually redact these details and provide images or transcripts of the pages relating to your ancestor on payment of a fee; these costs vary from repository to repository. Remember that if you are granted permission to see closed medical records, you must check with the archive if you are planning to publish the clinical information contained within them online or in print, for example, on a website or blog, or in an article or book. Many archives have a rule that 100 years need to have passed since the events in question. It's always worth revisiting your research to take into account previously closed records that become available after 100 years.

THE COUNTY REGISTER

If your ancestor was sent to a private madhouse outside London in the late eighteenth or early nineteenth century, it's worth trying the County Register held at The National Archives. Catalogued under MH51/735, this is an alphabetical record of the proprietors of madhouses for the period 1798–1812 arranged by county; it also includes a list of patients at each one. There are forty-two proprietors in the register, together with 1,788 patients. However, pauper patients accommodated in private madhouses at the expense of their parishes are not named. Nor is the list of madhouses complete because it's known that patients were being treated at unlicensed establishments.

LUNACY PATIENTS' ADMISSION REGISTERS

Contrary to their title, these documents are not the same as the admission registers kept by individual asylums. Held by The National Archives and catalogued under MH 94, they are the original Patients' Admission Registers kept by the Lunacy Commission (1846–1913) and the Board of Control (1913–1960). They list the name and gender of the patient; the name of the hospital, asylum or licensed house; the date of

No. in order of Admission	Name		Private		Pauper		Date of Admission	Asylum		D
			M.	F.	M.	F.				
3068	Green	Elizabeth				1	11 Dec 46	Oxford		15
3082	Girling	George			1		15 Dec 46	Notts		22
3099	Green	Francis				1	18 Dec 46	Hanwell		14
3101	Goodship	William				1	18 Dec 46	Gloucester		3
3147	Garrett	Margaret				1	24 Dec 46	W. York		29
3154	Gill	Susannah		1			24 Dec 46	Liverpool		24
3162	Greenwood	Mary				1	26 Dec 46	W. York		17
3210	Gates	Sarah				1	1 Jany 47	Lancaster		4
3298	Gadd	Rose		1			15 Jany 47	St Lukes		21
3314	Gilbert	William				1	18 Jany 47	Stafford		5
3323	Gibson	John				1	20 Jany 47	Salop		7
3344	Green	John	1				22 Jany 47	Gloucester		10
3360	Gay	Jane				1	25 Jany 47	Norfolk		28
3382	Grant	Henry				1	27 Jany 47	Leicester		18

Entries on the left-hand page of the Lunacy Patients' Admission Register, 1846. (Image © Ancestry www.ancestry.co.uk, original document at The National Archives: Lunacy Patients' Admission Registers; Class: MH 94; Piece: 12) admission and of discharge or death of each patient; and if discharged, whether the patient was recovered, relieved or not improved.

These central registers were compiled from returns sent in from individual asylums in England and Wales; the registers were divided into metropolitan licensed houses, provincial licensed houses, and county asylums and hospitals. Some patients' diaries have also been retained as part of the series, which can provide extra information about the medical and legal circumstances of each case.

Ancestry has digitised part of the series of registers (1846–1912) and it's always worth trying this if you've 'lost' an ancestor on the census. The MH 94 registers are by no means complete as not all transfers between asylums were recorded; this was probably because of administrative errors by the local clerks who sent in their returns to the Lunacy Commissioners.

If you can't find your forebear on Ancestry's Lunacy Patients' Admission Registers index but you know he or she was definitely in an institution, there are a couple of other methods to try. You could try using a wildcard in the search box, for example, the first three letters of the surname plus an asterisk (Hig*). This search would bring up everyone whose surname starts with 'Hig'). Another option is to browse through the registers instead as they are arranged chronologically and alphabetically, which makes searching slightly easier.

SCOTLAND'S GENERAL REGISTER OF LUNATICS IN ASYLUMS

The equivalent record for Scotland is the General Register of Lunatics in Asylums beginning in 1858; this lists all patients in asylums, including those who were already there on 1 January 1858. Unlike England and Wales, the identification number usually remains the same throughout a patient's lifetime, for instance, if he or she was discharged and readmitted at a later date. The National Records of Scotland holds the originals for 1858–1978, catalogued under MC7/1-38. The General Register includes the name and number of every patient; gender and whether pauper or private; admission date and the name of the asylum; the date of discharge or death; whether recovered, relieved, not improved or incurable; where removed to; and any other observations.

For Scottish patients admitted after 1 January 1858, there are also detailed admission forms. These are called Notices of Admissions by the Superintendent of the Mental Institutions and cover the period 1858–1962; they are catalogued under MC2/1-1239 at the National Records of Scotland. The admission forms provide detailed information about the circumstances in which the patient was admitted, including the 'Supposed Cause', observations by two doctors and facts related by relatives and friends. There is also plenty of biographical information about the patient such as age, occupation, place of abode and whether they had experienced mental illness before.

Scottish Indexes (https://www.scottishindexes.com/mcsearch.aspx) has indexed the MC7 and MC2 records, which are over 100 years old; indexing is ongoing and will continue. You can search for free and download records for a small fee. There is also an excellent tutorial video explaining how to use these sources (http://www.scottishindexes.com/learninghealth.aspx).

Case Study: John Kerr
Delusions of grandeur were very common in people afflicted with various types of mania. Thirty-nine-year-old John Kerr was admitted to the Royal Edinburgh Asylum for the Insane on 9 May 1865. It was his first attack of mental illness but symptoms had started four years earlier. The diagnosis was mania and the supposed cause was irregularity and want of employment.

John was a gardener and at the time of his admission, he and his wife Marion were living in Industry Lane, Leith; they had three children, aged seventeen, fourteen and twelve. John's education was good, his disposition cheerful but reserved and he was of steady and industrious habits. He was not epileptic, suicidal nor dangerous but he was clearly suffering from various delusions about being heir to a fortune and was diagnosed with mania.

4105

(Copies.)

CERTIFICATE OF EMERGENCY.

(This Certificate shall be granted only in cases in which the urgency of the symptoms renders hazardous the delay necessary to procure a Second Medical Certificate.)

I, the undersigned, having already granted the Medical Certificate, No. 1, hereto annexed, to the effect that
is a (¹) hereby further certify that the Case
of the said is One of Emer-
gency, and I recommend the immediate removal of the said
to an Asylum accordingly.

Name,_____

Place of Abode,_____

DATED this day of one thousand eight
hundred and

(¹) Lunatic, or an insane person, or an idiot, or a person of unsound mind.

ORDER TO BE GRANTED BY THE SHERIFF FOR THE TRANSMISSION AND RECEPTION OF THE LUNATIC.

I, *Patrick Arkley Esquire* (¹) *Sheriff Substitute*
of the (²) *County of Edinburgh*
having had produced to me, with a Petition at the instance of (³) *James Will*
Inspector of Poor, Errol
Certificates under the hands of *Francis J. White M R C P Edin*
and *James Wylie M R C S, Esq* , being two Medical Persons
duly qualified in terms of an Act, intituled "An Act for the Regulation of the Care and Treatment of Lunatics, and for the Provision, Maintenance, and Regulation of Lunatic Asylums in Scotland," setting forth that they had separately visited and examined (⁴)
Elspeth Weighton a Pauper and that the said
Elspeth Weighton is a (⁵) *person of unsound mind*
and a proper Person to be detained and taken care of, DO HEREBY AUTHORIZE you to receive the said *Elspeth Weighton* as a Patient into the
(⁶) *private* Asylum of *Millholme House* and I authorize
Transmission to the said Asylum accordingly ; and I transmit you herewith the said Medical Certificates, and a Statement regarding the said *Elspeth Weighton* which accompanied the said Petition.

(SIGNED) *P. Arkley*

DATED this *1st* day of *March* one thousand eight
hundred and *fifty eight*
To the Superintendent of the (⁷) *Private*
Asylum of *Millholme House*

(¹) State whether Sheriff, Sheriff-Substitute, Steward, or Steward-Substitute.
(²) State whether a County or Stewartry.
(³) Insert Name and Designation.
(⁴) Describe him, and if a Pauper, state so.
(⁵) Lunatic, or an Insane Person, or an Idiot, or a Person of unsound mind.
(⁶) Public, District, or Private, &c.
(⁷) Public, District, or Private, &c.

---

20 & 21 Vict., Cap. 71, Sect. 37.

NOTICE OF ADMISSION.

I HEREBY GIVE NOTICE, That (¹) *Mr George Patrick Baillie*
was received into this House as a (²)
private Patient on the *first* (³) day of *March*
and I hereby transmit a Copy of the Order and Medical Certificates and Statement on which he was received.

Subjoined is a Report with respect to the mental and bodily condition of the above-named Patient.

(SIGNED) _____ Superintendent.

DATED at *Bridgend* this *12th* (⁴) day of
March one thousand eight hundred and *fifty eight*

To the Secretary of the
General Board of Lunacy.

REPORT.

I HAVE this day (⁴) seen and personally examined *Mr George Patrick Baillie*
the Patient named in the above Notice,
and hereby report and certify, with respect to *his* mental state, that (⁵) *his*
mental condition is that of imbecility

and with respect to *his* bodily health and condition, that (⁶) *it appears*
sound

(SIGNED) _____

(⁷) *Resident Physician*
DATED this *12th* day of *March* one thousand eight
hundred and *fifty eight*

(¹) Name and Designation.
(²) Private or Pauper.
(³) Some day within fourteen days after the date of the Order of the Sheriff; or within twenty-one days, if the Order be granted by the Sheriff of Orkney and Shetland.
(⁴) Some day not less than two clear days after the admission of the Patient, and before the expiration of fourteen clear days after admission.
(⁵) Insert particulars.
(⁶) Insert particulars.
(⁷) Add Designation.

[⁴*]

The first page of George Patrick Baillie's Notice of Admission to Saughton Hall private asylum near Edinburgh in 1858. (© Emma Maxwell – National Records of Scotland Reference MC2/3 No. 4105 www.nrsscotland.gov.uk)

The second page of George Patrick Baillie's Notice of Admission to Saughton Hall private asylum near Edinburgh in 1858. (© Emma Maxwell – National Records of Scotland Reference MC2/3 No. 4105 www.nrsscotland.gov.uk)

According to the medical certificates, Marion had 'noticed a gradual change in him and for the last twelve months his delusions have been getting stronger. He fancies his neighbours are injuring him.' The two doctors who certified John was insane noticed he had a 'restless and wandering eye'.

After John had been admitted to the asylum, a more precise diagnosis was made: monomania of suspicion. In the first casebook entry, more details of John's delusions emerge: 'On admission he was quiet and somewhat averse to speak. He said that he was the rightful proprietor of estates in Haddington and Ayrshire and that there was a good deal of money in America which would fall to him. He also said that he was heir to George Heriot (who built the hospital). He was, however, very cautious not to commit himself too far. He was heir to George Heriot only if that George Heriot was a particular George Heriot whom he had in view.'

Several days after admission, the subject of his prosperity was again broached, but 'he refused to speak about it as he thought the information was desired only to make his detention more certain. He took up the idea that the reporter [note-taker] had been the means of getting him placed in the asylum, and in revenge he threatened to knock his (the reporter's) brains out. When it was explained that he had been sent here by warrant of the Sheriff, he got quite pacified.'

A few weeks later, John had been working in the garden but was 'very reserved and inclined to regard persons with suspicion'. He still had his wits about him because in July, it was reported that he had 'managed to leave the grounds and get into town, but was speedily brought back'.

There was no change in his mental state over the next twelve months. By September 1866, the case notes record that he 'will not work and never speaks, unless addressed – when he turns haughtily round and asks with an oath, what you have to do with him or any of the men here – that he is in charge of them – that he is a Government man. Walks round & round the airing court in a stiff erect manner, without moving his head to one side or the other – or apparently taking any notice of what is going on.'

Six months later, John was described as being 'pleasanter & more civil & more disposed to talk'; otherwise, there was no change in his mental state. By June 1867, he was working well in the garden but still considered the grounds round the asylum as his own property. There were regular monthly entries that simply stated 'no change' most of the time.

In June 1873, John was still working well independently but 'was discovered to be in possession of a key – which he gave up without making a disturbance'. By April 1876, John was on parole in the grounds doing 'a little work' but he still had 'delusions of an extravagant nature'. His bodily health was good.

John's wife Marion died in 1879 but there is no mention of this in the records. By 1882, he was still working on parole but was labouring 'under delusions respecting sin' and 'muttering to himself'.

In January 1883, the medical officer wrote that John was 'always pale notwithstanding he is on extras & has had haematinics'. This was medication to treat anaemia. By 1 April, John had been confined to bed for about three weeks because he was now suffering from general anasarca [edema]. Cardiac disease had been diagnosed. On 7 April, John died suddenly as a result of cardiac disease (duration unknown). He was aged fifty-seven and had been a patient in the asylum for almost eighteen years.

Sources: General Register of Lunatics in Asylums (MC7/2) and Notices of Admissions by the Superintendent of the Mental Institutions (MC2/82); at National Records of Scotland and online at Scottish Indexes (www.scottishindexes.com).

Royal Edinburgh Hospital Casebooks (LHB7/51/16, LHB7/51/18, LHB7/51/21 and LHB7/51/23); Royal Edinburgh Hospital Register of Death (LHB7/42/1); at Lothian Health Services Archive.

(With thanks to Lesley West for this information about her ancestor, and to National Records of Scotland, Scottish Indexes and Lothian Health Services Archive for permission to quote from John Kerr's records.)

ASYLUM RECORDS
Asylums kept three main types of record: admission registers, discharge registers, and patient casebooks and/or case files. The documents are more detailed from the 1840s onwards when a standard format was introduced. Bear in mind that asylums did not always use the printed forms in the way in which they were intended. For example, Bethlem did not include anything in the 'Sex and Class/Private' column about their patients, other than their gender.

ADMISSION REGISTERS
The admission registers include the full name, age and marital status of the patient; place of abode and occupation; date of admission and social class (pauper or private); mental and physical condition; the mental disorder the patient was suffering from; plus their religion and education. The name of the person who had agreed to the patient being certified before going to the asylum is also provided; this was usually a relative.

The admission registers state whether the patient was recovered, relieved or not improved on discharge. Sometimes more detail is given in the relevant discharge registers. Victorian lunatic asylums aimed to cure the mentally ill, wherever possible. For many patients, their well-being could be significantly improved by spending time away from their problems with regular food and work therapy.

The information about when symptoms of mental illness had first been spotted is useful. If it was months or sometimes years earlier, this implies that family members had been attempting to look after your ancestor. Having their mentally afflicted relative admitted to an asylum would doubtless have been a last resort, and the decision was probably only reached when they could no longer cope.

The column headed 'Name and address of relative to whom notice of death is to be sent' was completed by all asylums for a similar reason to the information provided for 'Next of kin' today. It

25.

ASYLUM REGISTER

Date of last previous Admission (if any).	No. in order of Admission.	Date of Admission.	Christian Name and Surname at full length.	Private M.	Private F.	Pauper M.	Pauper F.	Age.	Married.	Single.	Widowed.	Condition of Life and previous Occupation.	Previous Place of Abode.	County or Parish to which chargeable.	By whose Authority sent.
28ᵗʰ June 1894	2611	3ᵈ April 1895	Alexander Crichton		1			21		1		Farm Labourer	Balkhead of Thornton	Kinglassie Trans'ferred to Abdie.	Thos. M. Gray Sheriff Substitute
	2612	5ᵗʰ April 1895	Isabella Moyes				1	26		1		Domestic Servant	South Back Lochgelly more way	Auchterderran Transferred to Aberdour	Thos. M. Gray Sheriff Substitute
	2613	8ᵗʰ April 1895	John Arnott			1		72			1	Weaver	Kennoway	Kennoway	A.E. Henderson Sheriff Substitute
	2614	8ᵗʰ April 1895	Elizabeth Scott				1	57		1		No occupation	Dunshalt, Auchtermuchty	Auchtermuchty	A.E. Henderson Sheriff Substitute
20ᵗʰ Jany 1873	2615	8ᵗʰ April 1895	Andrew Ferguson			1		58	1			Miner	Lochgelly	Auchterderran	A.E. Henderson Sheriff Substitute
	2616	11ᵗʰ April 1895	James Harvey			1		34	1			Coal Miner	Park street, Cowdenbeath	Beath	A.E. Henderson Sheriff Substitute
	2617	22ᵈ April 1895	Matilda Sheach				1	51	1			Weaver	Collessie	Collessie	A.E. Henderson Sheriff Substitute
9ᵗʰ May 1887	2618	26ᵗʰ April 1895	David Morris			1		36	1			Miner	Lumphinnans Dunfermline Prison	Beath (Papers signed by Inspector of Poor, Dunfermline)	Sam: David Sheriff Substitute
	2619	5ᵗʰ May 1895	John Williamson			1		25		1		Factory-worker	Skene Sq, Strathmiglo	Strathmiglo	Thos. M. Gray Sheriff Substitute
	2620	6ᵗʰ May 1895	Elizabeth Clark				1	61		1		Hawker	Kirkcaldy Combination Poorhouse	Auchtermuchty	Thos. M. Gray Sheriff Substitute

A page from the Fife and Kinross District Asylum Register of Lunatics for April 1895. (Image © Ancestry www.ancestry.co.uk, original source: Fife and Kinross District Asylum Registers, Fife Library and Archives Services, Fife, Scotland)

OF LUNATICS.

Dates of Medical Certificates and by whom signed.	Bodily Condition.	Name of Disorder (if any).	Form of Mental Disorder.	Supposed Cause of Insanity.	Epileptics.	Congenital Idiots.	Duration of Existing attacks.			Number of previous attacks	Age on first attack.	Date of Discharge, Removal, or Death.	Discharged.			Died.	OBSERVATIONS.
							Years.	Months.	Weeks.				Recovered.	Relieved.	Not Improved.		
..D. Hay, M.B., C.M. April 1895 R. Turnbull M.B. Edin April 1895	Average		Mania	None known					about a week	2	19	22ⁿᵈ June 1895			1		Alexander Crichton, Bank head of Thornton, – father
..m Gellatly L.F.P.S. April 1895 ..mb Deuchle M.B. C.M. Edin April 1895	Weak		Mania	Not known					a few days	0	–	8ᵗʰ Nov 1895			1		Ebenezer Moyes, Smith Carmore, Lochgelly, – father
..Andrew, M.B. C.M. April 1895 R. Turnbull M.B. Edin April 1895	Fair	Varicose veins on both legs.	Mania	Alcoholism					about three weeks	0	–	1ˢᵗ May 1895			1		John Arnot, shoemaker, Low Lotgo, – son
F. MacDonald M.B. C.M. April 1895 R. Turnbull M.B. Edin April 1895	Average		Melan- cholia	Unknown				about three months		0	–	17ᵗʰ June 1895.				1	Mrs Wm Donaldson, Dunshle – sister.
..m Gellatly L.F.P.S. April 1895 ..mb Deuchle M.B. C.M. April 1895	Average		Mania	Death of grandchildren					a week or two	not known 1	about 25	28ᵗʰ Sept 1895			1		Elizabeth Finlay or Ferguson 56 High Street, Lochgelly, wife
..Thomson M.B. C.M. April 1895 ..Turnbull M.B. Edin April 1895	Weak	Has Bathing pulmonalis	Mania	Not known					a few days	0	–	24ᵗʰ May 1895			1		Mrs Margt Scott or Harvey Park St, Cowdenbeath, wife.
R. Turnbull M.B. Edin April 1895 ..Neaville M.B. C.M. April 1895 ..pory Certified m.B. Bell, M.B. C.M.)	Average		Mania	Unknown					2 weeks	1	50	17ᵗʰ May 1925				1	Mrs Smith, Collessie, – sister.
..m Luke M.B. C.M. April 1895 J. MacGregor M.B. C.M. Edin April 1895	Average		Mania	Uncertain			Uncertain			2	–	1ˢᵗ April 1914				1	John Morris, labourer, Otterston by Aberdour, – brother
..m Hogan M.B. C.P.S. May 1895 ..Turnbull M.B. Edin May 1895	Weak	Impaired perceptions harsh breath no abs pices of both lungs	Melan- cholia	Death of his father					Ten days	0	25	5ᵗʰ Sept 1895				1	Euphemia Williamson, Strathmiglo, – sister
..Welsh M.D. May 1895 R. Turnbull M.B. Edin May 1895	Weak	Considerable motor hom slowness the fracture of lower end of Humerus in ..phicating the Elbow joint	Mania	Drink					One week	0	61	11ᵗʰ July 1895				1	Andrew Clark, S.S.C., ... – brother.

165

was not because a high proportion of patients were expected to die; the information was recorded as a matter of course. The details are often the same as those given in the 'previous place of abode' and 'by whose authority sent' columns.

Not all patients were 'certified'; after 1890, an increasing number were classed as 'voluntary' and had requested treatment in an asylum, perhaps recognising the symptoms of a previous attack of mental illness.

CASEBOOKS AND CASE FILES

One of the most frustrating things about tracing an ancestor who spent time in a lunatic asylum is the gaps in coverage of casebooks or case files. This may mean that your ancestor's file is missing, although there might be a series of casebooks before and after the period you're interested in.

If you are lucky and your forebear's casebook has survived, you are likely to find regular reports about his or her health, behaviour and treatment in the asylum. From the 1870s onwards, there may also be photographs of patients. However, for those who were long-stay patients, the information provided may be disappointingly little. As the years passed, the medical officer may only have recorded an annual note of 'no change' in the file. Generally, there will be more detail in the first few years of admission and in the period immediately before discharge or death.

DISCHARGE REGISTERS

These documents are very useful for finding out where your ancestor was sent after discharge from a particular asylum. He or she may have been sent home into the care of their family or friends, transferred to another institution or sent to convalesce at a different facility. Your forebear could also have died while a patient there, either as a result of their mental illness or after contracting another disease.

If your mentally ill ancestor needed long-term care, you might find he or she was transferred to a different asylum, sometimes several times. There could be several reasons for this, depending on whether they were a private or pauper patient. If they had been sent to an asylum by a Poor Law union, money was usually the issue. Another possibility is that your forebear was being moved from an overcrowded institution to one that was not overly full. If a patient had reached a plateau in terms of their recovery and the medical superintendent believed he or she would benefit from treatment at another asylum, he would arrange for a transfer. The families of private patients might request to move their relative to another institution if they were dissatisfied with the level of care or treatment provided.

Case Study: William Mansfield

With a proud mining heritage, South Wales has had its fair share of pit disasters down the centuries. Somerset-born William Stanton Mansfield and his 15-year-old son Charles were survivors of a coal mining accident at the Prince of Wales Colliery in Abercarn, Monmouthshire, which killed nearly 270 men and boys, and more than fifty horses. William and Charles had been working as stonemasons in the pit.

On 11 September 1878, a fearful explosion occurred at midday. According to *The Graphic*, 'from every house in the village, and from every workshed and office, men, women and children, horrified at the sound and at the sight, rushed down the steep streets and hillsides towards the pit's mouth, screaming, shrieking and waving their hands.' The feeling of terror experienced by William's wife Betsey and their four other children waiting above ground would have been nothing compared with those trapped in the pit. A search party was sent down and 'after being repeatedly driven back by the foul gas', they reached a part of the mine where eighty-two men and boys were found alive, and mostly uninjured; they proved to be the sole survivors of the disaster, which was caused by firedamp exploding.

The horror of what William and Charles had experienced in such a traumatic event would undoubtedly have had an effect on them over the years. It was not, however, the reason that 45-year-old William became a patient in the Joint Counties Lunatic Asylum at Abergavenny some twelve years later. In January 1890, he was admitted there because he was suffering with symptoms of 'paralysis of the insane' (tertiary stage syphilis) and organic disease of the brain/intemperance. At the time of the 1881 census, William was still working as a stone mason but also running the Blacksmith's Arms in Clawrplwyf, Mynyddyslwyn. Perhaps his intemperance came hand in hand with the job; perhaps it was a way of dealing with his demons from the mining accident.

Whatever the reason, William's symptoms of mental illness had begun three years earlier. The disease progressed and as with all advanced cases of general paralysis of the insane, hospitalisation was required. It would have been too difficult and too distressing for Betsey to nurse her husband at home. On the 1891 census, she had three children aged eleven, eight and five to look after. An older son aged eighteen was still at home working as a collier, so he was probably able to contribute to the household income. Betsey also had two lodgers living with the family who would have provided some much needed extra money to help make up for William's missing wage.

William's case is typical of the kind of frustrations that can be encountered when tracing an ancestor in a lunatic asylum. Although he was admitted in 1890, there are no surviving case notes for him prior to 1899 so it is not possible to find out the state of his health on admission. In February 1899, the notes simply say, 'Suffers from dementia, is quite unable to converse'. By October, William was 'very simple' and 'cannot converse rationally'. On 31 December 1899, it was recorded that he was suffering from inflammation of the left lung. He was treated with expectorants and stimulants but he was 'very restless' with an evening temperature of 104°; by the morning, it was just a few degrees lower. By 2 January 1900, William's temperature was still up but he was taking a fair amount of liquid food. However, his heart was failing and he was resting badly; two days later, he died. The asylum recorded that the cause of death was bronchitis but on his death certificate, it is noted as pneumonia.

Sources: Joint Counties Lunatic Asylum, Abergavenny Patient Admission Register (D3202/30/6) and Male Case Record Book (D3202/40/10); at Gwent Archives.

(With thanks to Linda Cooke for this information about her ancestor and to Gwent Archives for permission to quote from William Stanton Mansfield's records.)

ANNUAL REPORTS

At first glance, you might think annual reports of lunatic asylums make dry reading but they can actually tell you a great deal about the institution in which your ancestor was detained. Although patients won't be named, the reports provide an interesting overview of each year. For example, you're likely to find out whether there were any building works to improve the site; if there had been any notable epidemics affecting the patients; and how many patients had been under restraint, for what reason and by which method. There will usually also be extracts from the latest visit by the Lunacy Commissioners.

Most importantly, the annual reports will tell you the name of the Medical Superintendent and Assistant Medical Officer. You can then search for them in newspaper articles or on the internet to find out what their philosophy was regarding the treatment of the mentally ill and whether they had pioneered any specific methods. Senior members of staff will also be listed. Don't just look at a few reports; try to read as many as you can for the period in which your ancestor was at the asylum because treatments and living conditions did change over time.

The best place to see annual reports from lunatic asylums online is The Medical Heritage Library on the Internet Archive

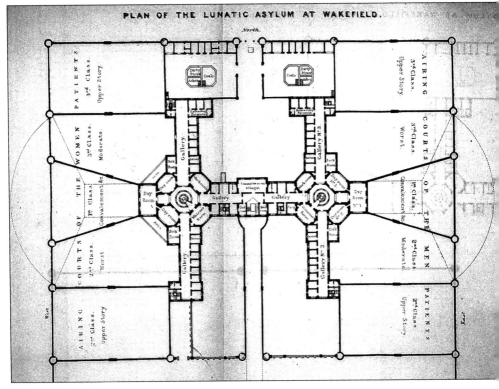

Plan of Wakefield Lunatic Asylum, 1841. (Wellcome Collection. CC BY)

(https://archive.org/details/medicalheritagelibrary). Under 'Topics and Subjects', you can narrow down the results by ticking 'Hospitals, Psychiatric'. You can also filter by creator (the name of the institution) and by year.

Other asylum records that are useful for getting an overview of an institution are visiting committee minutes, photographs and architectural plans.

REPORTS OF LUNACY COMMISSIONERS
The correspondence and papers of the Lunacy Commission (later the Board of Control) catalogued under MH 51 are held at The

National Archives. Generally, the information contained in the documents is not about individuals, but focuses on advice to lunatic asylums and on conditions within specific institutions. Search Discovery to find out more (http://discovery.nationalarchives.gov. uk/).

BETHLEM HOSPITAL ARCHIVE

If your ancestor was admitted to Bethlem, either as a mentally ill patient or as a criminal lunatic, you might be able to find his or her records in the Bethlem Hospital Archive. This rich collection of documents is a real treasure trove of information about the treatment and lives of patients at the hospital, some of which have been digitised on Find My Past. The remainder can be consulted at the Bethlem Museum of the Mind Archive by appointment; see the website for further details (https://museumofthemind.org.uk/ collections/archives). The archive also includes the records of Warlingham Park Hospital, previously Croydon Mental Hospital.

For mentally ill patients, the main series of records are the general admission registers (reference ARA) from 1683 to 1973, digitised up to 1902; the patient discharge, transfer and/or death registers and lists (reference DDR) from 1782 to 1991, digitised up to 1906; and the patient casebooks (reference CB) for 1778 to 1947, digitised up to 1919.

There are also incurable patient admission registers 1723–1919 (reference ARB); female voluntary patient admission registers 1890–1910 for those who were uncertified (reference ARC); Croydon Mental Hospital male and female patient casebooks 1903–1913 (reference CWA); and Croydon Mental Hospital male and female private patient casebooks 1903–1913 (reference CWB).

At Bethlem, pauper patients were not admitted after 1857 because there were plenty of public asylums in London for the poor. In the admission registers, the initials 'P. P.' in the sureties column denotes 'Private Patient'. Some people paid a deposit on admission, which was refunded when they were discharged; this is abbreviated to 'Dep.' in the registers. There were no fees because Bethlem was a charitable institution. Non-private patients were usually drawn from the middle classes.

The entry that states 'See authority' was a cross-reference from the admission books to the admission forms, which comprised the legal authority for admission. Bethlem's patient admission papers (reference BAP) have not been digitised.

To follow the trail of where your ancestor went after being discharged from Bethlem, check the details in the discharge registers, which have also been digitised. Sometimes patients were sent back to their own homes or to live with relatives who could look after them; sometimes they were transferred to another asylum, either at Bethlem's or the family's request; or after 1870, to Bethlem's convalescence facility at Witley in rural Surrey.

For criminal lunatics, there is a useful series of criminal patient admission registers (reference ARD) for 1816–1864; these have been digitised on Find My Past. These include details of admission date; name, age, address or previous institution; crime, verdict, when and where tried; condition of life; and discharge or removal date.

The other records for criminal lunatics have not been digitised so you will need to visit the Bethlem Archive to view the relevant documents. The incurable and criminal patient casebooks (reference CBC) for 1816–1864 contain case notes about the health and treatment of patients. There are also reception warrants (reference CRW) for 1816–1864 and discharge warrants (reference CDW) for 1817–1864; both of these types of document were issued by the Secretary of State, not Bethlem.

The hospital was required to produce quarterly reports on the criminal lunatics it cared for; these are catalogued under 'criminal resolutions, correspondence and returns' (reference CSA) from 1810 to 1885; a small number of criminal lunatics remained at Bethlem after 1864 when the majority were sent to Broadmoor, which is why the returns continued. There are also gaol returns of criminals transferred to Bethlem (reference GR) from 1816 to 1850; these records provide details about each criminal's crime, trial, character and health.

BROADMOOR ARCHIVE

The historic records of Broadmoor Hospital, formerly Broadmoor Criminal Lunatic Asylum, are held at Berkshire Record Office. You can view the rules for access to the records in this PDF (http://www.berkshirerecordoffice.org.uk/storage/app/media/pdfs/B RO-BH-protocol.pdf). You can also search the Berkshire Record Office catalogue to find out what records are available (http://www.berkshirerecordoffice.org.uk/search-catalogue).

CHANCERY LUNATICS

Like wills and probate, the records of Chancery lunatics can be difficult to trace. Check the national research guides for more information. For England and Wales, try The National Archives guide to 'Chancery Equity Suits 1558–1875' (http://www.nationalarchives. gov.uk/help-with-your-research/research-guides/chancery-equity-suits-after-1558/). For Scotland, check the National Records of Scotland guide to 'Chancery Records' (https://www.nrscotland.gov. uk/research/guides/chancery-records).

POOR LAW RECORDS

If your ancestor was in a workhouse or poorhouse before being admitted to a lunatic asylum, it's worth checking to see if there are relevant Poor Law records. Where they have survived, there may be admission and discharge registers, reception orders, documents about restraint, minutes of the Board of Guardians or registers of lunatics. Some workhouse records are online; Ancestry's London Poor Law collection is a good example. However, for most, you'll need to visit the relevant archive to view the records. Search Discovery for England and Wales (http://discovery.nationalarchives. gov.uk/), the Scottish Archive Network for Scotland (https://www.

scan.org.uk), or the Public Record Office of Northern Ireland (https://www.nidirect.gov.uk/proni).

PRISON RECORDS

If your ancestor was found not guilty of a crime by reason of insanity, he or she was a criminal lunatic. There should be trial and prison records relating to the case, which will tell you more. Start with Find My Past's Crime, Prisons and Punishment collection, which includes criminal registers (HO 27) 1805–1892; quarterly returns from convict hulks, convict prisons and convict lunatic asylums (HO 8) 1801–1854; and calendars of prisoners (HO 140) 1868–1929.

You could also check the Criminal Lunacy Warrant and Entry Books (HO 145) 1882–1898 and the Criminal Lunatic Asylum Registers (HO 20) 1820–1843, which are on Ancestry. A growing number of prison records are also online, for example, Gloucestershire, Somerset and Cornwall are on Ancestry.

MILITARY LUNATICS

Only a few records have survived for military lunatics, such as those for Haslar, catalogued under ADM 305 and held at The National Archives. They include a journal of the lunatic asylum 1830–1842 (ADM 305/102) and a muster book for 1863 with a list of lunatics accommodated at Haywards Heath (ADM 305/87). There are a few other records relating to Hoxton House, Haslar and Yarmouth in ADM 102 and ADM 105. Unfortunately, no records of patients at the Royal Victoria Hospital, Netley have survived.

ONLINE SOURCES

An increasing number of asylum records have been digitised online, and more and more will appear as time passes. Find My Past has the Bethlem Hospital Patient Admission Registers & Casebooks (1683–1932); it also has transcripts for Prestwich Asylum Admissions (1851–1901), South Yorkshire Asylum Admissions (1872–1910) and Bexley Asylum Minute Books (1901–1939).

Rubery Asylum, Staffordshire, circa 1900. (Author's collection)

Ancestry has digitised the Criminal Lunacy Warrant and Entry Books (1882–1898) and some early Criminal Lunatic Asylum Registers (1820–1843); the originals are held at The National Archives. The Ancestry website also has the Lunacy Patients Admission Registers (1846–1912), as well as indexes of the registers for inmates at St Lawrence's Asylum, Bodmin, Cornwall (1840–1900) and Fife and Kinross Asylum Registers (1866–1937).

Ancestry has also digitised the London, Poor Law and Board of Guardian records (1738–1930). Within this collection are documents associated with pauper lunatics such as registers of lunatics accommodated at particular asylums and reception orders.

Powick Asylum Patients' records are on the Worcester Medical Museums website and can be accessed via a searchable database (https://medicalmuseum.org.uk/powick-patients/?rq=asylum). History to Herstory (http://www.historytoherstory.org.uk) has digitised some casebooks for females at West Riding Pauper Lunatic Asylum.

The Wellcome Library and its partnership archives are continuing to digitise records for key UK psychiatric institutions. Currently accessible are Ticehurst House Hospital, East Sussex; The Retreat, York; Gartnavel Royal Hospital (Glasgow Lunatic Asylum); St Luke's Hospital, London; Holloway Sanatorium, Surrey; Crichton Royal Hospital, Dumfries & Galloway; Camberwell House Asylum, Surrey; Priory Hospital, London; and Manor House Asylum, London. More material will be added when available. You can search the collections at www.wellcomelibrary.org/collections/digital-collections/mental-healthcare.

The way the records have been digitised replicates exactly how you would look at them in an archive. They are not searchable by name but you can browse whole registers and some can be downloaded as PDFs for future reference. However, don't just rely on digitised records as you're likely to end up missing part of the puzzle. Wherever possible, you should try to access your ancestor's asylum records.

Appendix 1

TERMINOLOGY IN LUNATIC ASYLUM RECORDS

Airing court	a defined area of an asylum's grounds used for exercise and recreation
Aural hallucinations	usually hearing voices of invisible people
Certified	a patient found insane after examination by medical practitioners and 'certified' as being so
Chancery lunatic	a patient found lunatic by inquisition
Criminal lunatic	a patient found not guilty of a crime on the grounds of insanity and detained indefinitely in an asylum
Demented	mentally unbalanced through intense emotion such as anger or grief
Dipsomania	a temporary form of insanity caused by drunkenness
Ep.	an abbreviation for 'epileptic', often used with mania
Fatuous	in a state of idiocy or imbecility
GPI	an abbreviation for 'general paralysis of the insane'
Parole	convalescent patients were 'on parole' before their discharge when allowed to go out by themselves
Partial insanity	another term for monomania

Pauper patient	before 1930, a patient whose treatment was paid for by the parish or Poor Law union
Private patient	a patient whose treatment was paid for by his or her family
Rate-aided	after 1930, a patient whose treatment was paid for by the state
Restraint	the use of mechanical means to control a violent patient
Seclusion	being forcibly placed in a locked room for a period of time
Service patient	an ex-serviceman whose asylum fees were paid by the Ministry of Pensions
Single lunatic	a patient confined in a house where no other lunatics were kept
Strong clothes	garments made of very strong material to prevent a violent patient from tearing them
Voluntary patient	someone who was not certified but requested asylum treatment
Wet and dirty	a patient who was doubly incontinent

Appendix 2

USEFUL WEBSITES

Andrew Roberts' Mental Health History Timeline
http://studymore.org.uk/mhhtim.htm

The Workhouse
http://www.workhouses.org.uk/

Bethlem Museum of the Mind (floorplan)
http://learning.museumofthemind.org.uk/explore-bethlem

County Asylums
https://www.countyasylums.co.uk/

Historic Hospitals: An Architectural Gazetteer
https://historic-hospitals.com

The National Archives Research Guide on Mental Health
http://www.nationalarchives.gov.uk/help-with-your-research/research-guides/mental-health/

Scottish Indexes
https://www.scottishindexes.com/learninghealth.aspx

The Science Museum
http://broughttolife.sciencemuseum.org.uk/broughttolife/objects

Netley Military Cemetery
https://www.netley-military-cemetery.co.uk/hospital-buildings/the-asylum-d-block-e-block-and-p-wing/

The Internet Archive
https://archive.org

Google Books
https://books.google.co.uk/

Appendix 3

PLACES TO VISIT

Bethlem Museum of the Mind
Bethlem Royal Hospital, Monks Orchard Road, Beckenham BR3 3BX
https://museumofthemind.org.uk/

Glenside Hospital Museum, Bristol
The Chapel in UWE Glenside Campus, Blackberry Hill, Stapleton, Bristol BS16 1DD
http://www.glensidemuseum.org.uk/

Kent County Lunatic Asylum (Oakwood Hospital) grounds
St Andrews Road, Maidstone, Kent ME16 9AN
Now converted to apartments but you can explore the landscaped grounds to view the Grade II listed buildings.
https://www.atlasobscura.com/places/kent-county-lunatic-asylum-oakwood-hospital

Mental Health Museum, Fieldhead Hospital, Wakefield
Mental Health Museum, Fieldhead, Ouchthorpe Lane, Wakefield WF1 3SP
https://www.southwestyorkshire.nhs.uk/mental-health-museum/home/

Mendip Hospital Cemetery, Wells
Hooper Avenue, Wells, Somerset BA5 3NA
One of the UK's few surviving asylum cemeteries.
http://mendiphospitalcemetery.org.uk/

Wellcome Collection
183 Euston Road, London NW1 2BE
https://wellcomecollection.org/

BIBLIOGRAPHY

Andrews, Jonathan, Briggs, Asa, Porter, Roy, Tucker, Penny & Waddington, Keir, *A History of Bethlem*, Routledge, 1997.

Arnold, Catherine, *Bedlam: London and Its Mad*, Simon & Schuster, 2008.

Battie, William, *A Treatise on Madness*, J. Whiston & B. White, 1758.

Browne, Alexander Francis, *What Asylums Were, Are and Ought to Be, Being the Substance of Five Lectures Delivered to the Managers of the Montrose Lunatic Asylum*, Adam & Charles Black, 1837.

Burtinshaw, Kathryn & Burt, John, *Lunatics, Imbeciles and Idiots: A History of Insanity in Nineteenth Century Britain and Ireland*, Pen & Sword, 2017.

Busfield, Joan, *Managing Madness: Changing Ideas and Practice*, Routledge, 1986.

Chater, Kathy, *My Ancestor Was a Lunatic: A Guide to Sources for Family Historians*, Society of Genealogists, 2014.

Cherry, Steven, *Medical Services and the Hospitals in Britain 1860–1939*, Cambridge University Press, 1996.

Crammer, John, *Asylum History: Buckinghamshire County Pauper Lunatic Asylum – St John's*, The Royal College of Psychiatrists, 1990.

Crompton, Frank, *Doctor Sherlock's Casebook: Patients Admitted to the Worcester City and County Pauper Lunatic Asylum at Powick August 1854 to March 1881*, George Marshall Medical Museum, 2016.

Crompton, Frank, *Workhouse Children*, Sutton Publishing, 1997.

Crowther, M.A., *The Workhouse System 1834–1929*, The University of Georgia Press, 1981.

DeLacy, Margaret, *Prison Reform in Lancashire, 1700–1850: A Study in Local Administration*, Manchester University Press, 1986.

Digby, Anne, *Pauper Palaces*, Routledge & Kegan Paul, 1978.

Fowler, Simon, *Tracing Your First World War Ancestors: A Guide for Family Historians*, Pen & Sword Books, 2013.

Fowler, Simon, *Tracing Your Naval Ancestors: A Guide for Family Historians*, Pen & Sword Books, 2011.

Fraser, David (ed.), *The Christian Watt Papers*, Caledonian Books, 1988.

Gardner, James, *Sweet Bells Jangled Out of Tune: A History of the Sussex Lunatic Asylum (St Francis Hospital) Haywards Heath*, James Gardner, 1999.

Grogan, Suzie, *Shell Shocked Britain: The First World War's Legacy for Britain's Mental Health*, Pen & Sword Books, 2014.

Grundy, Joan E., *A Dictionary of Medical & Related Terms for the Family Historian*, Swansong Publications, 2006.

Halliday, Sir Andrew, *A General View of the Present State of Lunatics and Lunatic Asylums in Great Britain and Ireland*, Thomas & George Underwood, 1828.

Hamilton, David, *The Healers: A History of Medicine in Scotland*, Canongate, 1981.

Higgs, Michelle, *Life in the Victorian and Edwardian Workhouse*, The History Press, 2007.

Higgs, Michelle, *Life in the Victorian Hospital*, The History Press, 2009.

Higgs, Michelle, *Prison Life in Victorian England*, The History Press, 2007.

Lane, Joan, *A Social History of Medicine*, Routledge, 2001.

Lomax, Montagu, *The Experiences of an Asylum Doctor with Suggestions for Asylum and Lunacy Law Reform*, George Allen & Unwin Ltd, 1921.

Longmate, Norman, *The Workhouse*, Pimlico, 2003.

Mackenzie, Eneas, *Historical Account of Newcastle-upon-Tyne including the Borough of Gateshead*, Mackenzie & Dent, 1827.

McConville, Sean, *English Local Prisons 1860–1900: Next Only to Death*, Routledge, 1995.

Muyden, Madam Ban (trans. and ed.), *A Foreign View of England in the Reigns of George I & George II: The Letters of Monsieur César de Saussure to his Family*, E.P. Dutton & Company, 1902.

Parry-Jones, William, *The Trade in Lunacy: A Study of Private Madhouses in England in the Eighteenth and Nineteenth Centuries*, Routledge & Kegan Paul, 1972.

Perfect, William, *Select Cases in the Different Species of Insanity, Lunacy or Madness*, 1787.

Porter, Roy, *Madmen: A Social History of Madhouses, Mad-Doctors & Lunatics*, Tempus Publishing, 2004.

Porter, Roy, *Madness: A Brief History*, Oxford University Press, 2002.

Porter, Roy, 'Mental Illness' in Porter, Roy, (ed.), *The Cambridge Illustrated History of Medicine*, Cambridge University Press, 1996, pp.278–303.

Read, Charles Stanford, *Military Psychiatry In Peace and War*, H.K. Lewis & Co. Ltd, 1920.

Rutherford, Sarah, *The Victorian Asylum*, Shire Publications, 2008.

Scull, Andrew, *The Most Solitary of Afflictions: Madness and Society in Britain, 1700–1900*, Yale University Press, 1993.

Stallard, J.H., *Pauper Lunatics and their Treatment*, Longmans, Green & Co., 1870.

Stevens, Mark, *Broadmoor Revealed: Victorian Crime and the Lunatic Asylum*, Pen & Sword Books, 2013.

Stevens, Mark, *Life in the Victorian Asylum: The World of Nineteenth Century Mental Health Care*, Pen & Sword Books, 2014.

Stevenson, John, *British Society 1914–1945*, Penguin, 1998.

Thornbury, Walter, *Old and New London: A Narrative of Its History, Its People and Its Places*, Cassell, Petter, Galpin & Co., 1881.

Tuke, Daniel Hack, *Chapters in the History of the Insane in the British Isles*, Kegan Paul, Trench & Co., 1882.

Tuke, Samuel, *Description of the Retreat, an Institution near York for Insane Persons of the Society of Friends*, W. Alexander, 1813.

Wheeler, Ian, *Fair Mile Hospital: A Victorian Asylum*, The History Press, 2015.

Wise, Sarah, *Inconvenient People: Lunacy, Liberty and the Mad-Doctors in Victorian England*, Vintage Books, 2013.

ARTICLES IN PERIODICALS

Wilkinson, T.W., 'Lunatic London', *Living London*, 1902, Volume II, pp.338–43.

Dickens, Charles, 'A Walk in a Workhouse', *Household Words*, 25 May 1850.

Smith, L.D., 'Duddeston Hall and the Trade in Lunacy 1835–65', *Birmingham Historian*, 1992, Volume 8, pp.16–22.

Smith, Toni, 'Witches, Idiots, Imbeciles and Lunatics', *Your Family Tree*, November 2004, pp.42–5.

Stretton, Hesba, 'One of God's Palaces: The Royal Albert Asylum', *Sunday Magazine*, January 1885.

Topp, Leslie, 'Single Rooms, Seclusion and the Non-Restraint Movement in British Asylums, 1838–1844', *Social History of Medicine*, Volume 31, Issue 4, pp.754–73.

Williamson, Arthur, 'The Beginnings of State Care for the Mentally Ill in Ireland', *Economic and Social Review*, Volume 1, 1970, pp.281–90.

UNPUBLISHED THESES

Sturdy, Harriet C.G., *Boarding-out the insane, 1857–1913: a study of the Scottish system*, PhD thesis, 1996.

PERIODICALS AND NEWSPAPERS

Gentleman's Magazine
Illustrated London News
Lancaster Gazette
Norfolk Chronicle
The Graphic
The Penny Magazine
The Lancet
West Bromwich Free Press
Western Times

INDEX